PRAISE FOR

Who We Are Becoming Matters

A tone poem that touches ancestral wisdom to teach us how to meet the present moment. It's a meditation. Read slowly.

The Reverend Canon Mpho Tutu van Furth
Author of *Forgiveness and Reparation* and coauthor of *Made for Goodness*

Such an extraordinary voice of prose and poetry that demands the reader's attention. And what a profound and brilliant use of our attention. I am well-familiar with the teachings but I was riveted by Wong Roshi's style that woke me up. Thank you.

Margaret Wheatley
Author of several books, including *Restoring Sanity*, *Leadership and the New Science*, and *Who Do We Choose to Be?*

Who We Are Becoming Matters reads like an invitation; a set of gentle nudges to think and act in radically different ways. It is in part an analysis of the current state of the world and in part a series of reflections on how to improve one's daily practices so that life is better aligned with nature, ancestral wisdom and courageous dedication to a peaceful future. Activists, cultural workers, scholars, parents and spiritual leaders alike will find something in these pages that will affect our collective work to improve the human condition.

Dr. Beth E. Richie
Author of *Arrested Justice* and distinguished professor of criminology, law, and justice and Black studies and inaugural chair in the humanities and social sciences, University of Illinois at Chicago

The future of our species and all species depends not only on what we do, but who we are and who we evolve to become. Norma Wong gives us practical and inspiring guidance for how to show up in this timeplace of collapse of everything we think we know. A prophet for our time, she instructs us in the necessity and pleasure of meeting this moment in history wide awake—with courage, community, compassion, spaciousness, creativity, and wisdom.

Deepak Bhargava
President of The Freedom Together Foundation and coauthor of *Practical Radicals*

Wong Roshi's follow up to *When No Thing Works* is so timely and needed given the startling speed at which systems and institutions continue to collapse. *Who We Are Becoming Matters* offers volumes of wisdom in an accessible and engaging form. Norma reminds us, consciously and with great care, to take the time to shift our own patterns and habits and lean into the full gifts of our humanity. In doing so, she presents an alternative to the chaos, inviting us instead to seize the opportunity found in the path of aloha. An enthusiastic 999-33-7777 (see chapter 6) is my response when asked if you should read this stellar book. While sharing my enthusiastic book review over breakfast with my husband, he replied, "Ah, so this is not a how-to manual, it's a how-to-become manual."

Pam Omidyar
The Omidyar Group

Who We Are
Becoming Matters

Who We Are Becoming Matters

The Courage, Wisdom, and Aloha We Need in a Timeplace of Collapse

Norma Kawelokū Wong

North Atlantic Books
Huichin, unceded Ohlone land
Berkeley, California

North Atlantic Books
Huichin, unceded Ohlone land
2526 Martin Luther King Jr. Way
Berkeley, CA 94704 USA
www.northatlanticbooks.com

Cover art © AmkaArts via Shutterstock
Cover design by Jess Morphew
Book design by Happenstance Type-O-Rama

Printed in Canada

Who We Are Becoming Matters: The Courage, Wisdom, and Aloha We Need in a Timeplace of Collapse is sponsored and published by North Atlantic Books, an educational non-profit that collaborates with partners to develop cross-cultural perspectives; nurture holistic views of art, science, the humanities, and healing; and seed personal and global transformation by publishing work on the relationship of body, spirit, and nature.

North Atlantic Books's publications are distributed to the US trade and internationally by Penguin Random House Publisher Services. For further information, visit our website at *www.northatlanticbooks.com*.

The authorized representative in the EU for product safety and compliance is Eucomply OÜ, Pärnu mnt 139b-14, 11317 Tallinn, Estonia, hello@eucompliancepartner.com, +33757690241.

Library of Congress Cataloging-in-Publication Data

Names: Wong, Norma Ryūkō Kawelokū, 1956- author
Title: Who we are becoming matters : courage, wisdom, and aloha in the timeplace of collapse / Norma Ryūkō Kawelokū Wong Roshi.
Description: Huichin, unceded Ohlone land, Berkley, CA, USA : North Atlantic Books, [2025] | Summary: "Courage, Wisdom, and Aloha in the Timeplace of Collapse"-- Provided by publisher.
Identifiers: LCCN 2025019790 (print) | LCCN 2025019791 (ebook) | ISBN 9798889843214 paperback | ISBN 9798889843221 epub
Subjects: LCSH: Self-realization | Courage | Wisdom | Conduct of life
Classification: LCC BF637.S4 W66 2026 (print) | LCC BF637.S4 (ebook) | DDC 158--dc23/eng/20250918
LC record available at https://lccn.loc.gov/2025019790
LC ebook record available at https://lccn.loc.gov/2025019791

This book includes recycled material and material from well-managed forests.

1 2 3 4 5 6 7 8 9 FRIESENS 30 29 28 27 26

Acknowledgments

To ancestors—humans and not, for descendants—humans and not, with fellow practitioners and peace warriors of many paths, with much aloha I humbly acknowledge the makana, the gift, of our collective endeavors. Mahalo nui loa.

Contents

Foreword

Who We Are Becoming Matters: Courage, Wisdom, and Aloha in the Timeplace of Collapse reads like metaphysical slam poetry commenting on the chaos of our times, but rather than lamenting, asserts that Humanity will arise. It is Norma streaming her thoughts and good humor—as a Zen master, a Hawaiian spiritual teacher, and a political strategist—on our modern life and the planetary, political, and economic perils we are currently facing.

I have known Norma for more than forty years, first as students under Tanouye Tenshin Rotaishi at Chozen-ji. I was one of the young men training at the dojo, when Norma was struggling with illness and pain, who held her feet trying our best to put energy into her. Something must have worked, for Norma is now sixty-nine years old with hundreds of students all over the United States. She travels all the time to give talks and conduct *sesshin* (a six-day intensive training to collect the mind), truly the Energizer Bunny. As the abbot of Chozen-ji, I can only admire her tenacity and creativity as she develops her own approach to wisdom and compassion.

Norma's physical frailty did not allow her to do the normal, martial arts training at Chozen-ji, so Tanouye Rotaishi made the kitchen her dojo. She served coffee to his guests and saw him apply Sun Tzu's *Art of War* in his conversations with business and political leaders. She learned cooking from him, making food that was clear, satisfying, and accorded with the weather of the day.

In 2000 Tanouye Rotaishi created Anko-in as a sub-temple for women at Chozen-ji and made Norma its abbot. Today Anko-in is a Far-Flung Sangha with priests and students of all genders training all over, both online and at *sesshin*. Never one to follow norms, Norma created her own line of priest robes with a Chinese and Hawaiian flair. Her teachings are anchored in two great traditions, Zen Buddhism and Hawaiian spirituality, and she created a Hawaiian chant, *He Iwi Hilo*, from a poem inspired by the Heart Sutra. She has practiced setting flowers, calligraphy, cooking, and Dogi Kow Roshi's 10-Step Tai Chi for decades. All this has led to an approach that makes spirituality and Zen training accessible to many more people with its contemporary setting, warmth, and iconoclastic discipline.

Norma makes the daily activities of living into practice and in her book describes enough of her life in Kalihi in free-association-like detail that it is easy to imagine her day from the time of her rising, breaking her fast in her who-cares-what-she's-wearing clothes, and eventually sitting down to write, teacup in hand. If you put yourself in that same frame of mind, I think you will enjoy this book the most, a little at a time because it is so little after all, but skipping parts that go on too long.

In this timeplace of collapse, Norma declares that the imperative is to realize our Humanity, our interpenetrating Wholeness, for the sake of our existence on Earth. Mysteriously, wondrously, striving for this realization makes us each individually free and happy. The imperative is Aloha, the first and last word.

Aloha and Gassho,

Sayama Daian Roshi, Abbot of Chozen-ji

Preface

In my slim *When No Thing Works*, there is a tiny chapter on H_u — the Human Quotient of what's needed if humanity is to make it through to the other side of societal collapse and more than survive; indeed, to thrive. This book provides more detail of those few pages.

Who we are matters! This has always been so. Now, in a timeplace of expanding turmoil, even more so. Beyond ideas, policy, desires, and actions, human choices and behaviors depend on who we are and who we are determined to become. Beyond determination, are we willing to do the disciplined work necessary to interrupt the indulgences and habits that got us to this timeplace? The jury is out. Outcomes are consequential. Consequences matter!

Once more, I leap into the faith that something will meet the sincere inquiry of people I have not yet met and will likely never be with. Across timespace . . . if there is to be a leap, let it be now.

Me ka ha'aha'a, with humility, I wish you useful reading,

Norma Ryūkō Kawelokū Wong Roshi

CHAPTER 1

An Opening

My teacher taught me this. His name was Tanouye Tenshin Rotai-shi. He related the story of its origin. It has been proven to me over decades through observation and I have had no reason or data to doubt this learning. The origin story of its discovery? According to how my teacher learned it to be so and then passed on to me that it is so, the Chinese of the long and fruitful period of inquiry of the Tao gave birth to the hand-clasping ways of knowing.

Clasp your hands, as if in contemplation. (Go ahead and clasp your hands. Don't try to work this out in your head!) Is your left thumb over your right thumb, or is your right thumb over your left thumb? If your left thumb is over your right thumb, then you are primarily an emotional thinker—how something feels, how you feel about it, will be the immediate assessment pattern and how you land a decision, or not. If your right thumb is over your left thumb, then you are primarily a logical thinker—how things link and align, how you think about how it links and aligns, will be the immediate assessment pattern and how you land a decision, or not. Being a feeler doesn't mean you are absent of logic, and being a thinker doesn't strip you of emotion. As humans, we are unconsciously inclined toward one or the other and, for the most part, we are successfully served. Until we are not.

I, Norma Wong, kamaʻāina, born of these islands, am a logical thinker. Right thumb over left thumb and no doubt about it. This kind of knowing clicked in very early in life, as I will relate in some future chapter. By the time I had entered the ninth grade at Kamehameha Schools, there were many constructs and earnest bundles in my mind: how the islands might move on from the plantations and the military and the hotels; whether enough rain fell in Maunawili on one side of the range and Kalihi and Manoa on the other side of the range for a-l-l of the people to drink forever; what should it mean for those of us who look and think and act differently from those born on the continent to be this thing called an American. There were more minor constructs though nonetheless earnest bundles as well: why do the seniors have privileges, which the junior me wrote up in an editorial in the school newspaper and earned a few weeks of hazing; whether the JROTC program should become coed, and no longer mandatory for all four years for the boys, which I argued in favor of in Student Council and earned a lifetime of mostly principled debate with the then student body president who later went on to various prestigious elected offices from which we still debated various earnest things of hopefully more import.

From that early time onward, there was a continuous stream of unfolding puzzles filling most of every day, every week, every year without fatigue or despair.

And then one day I **felt** frustrated **without understanding why** it was so. And that moment—which to this day I remember in my very bones—was the beginning of the end.

The end?! The end of what?!

Before I get to that part, let me reassure you that this isn't just a musing for the thinkers of the world. In fact, my friend who is a tested and bona fide feeler, sorry—a bona fide emotional thinker,

2

has their own story of unraveling. It involves many stories of feeling their way (accompanied by hand placement on heart, or stomach, or on both sides of their head or someone else's head, and sometimes dramatic gestures to the sky of one hand or the other) through the twisted roads of life's momentous decisions. My friend usually glides energetically and happily in a stream of ups and downs that would soon tire me, the logical thinker. There was a lot of drama throughout the course of my friend's early and middle life that was also accompanied by productive bursts of creative enterprise in music and the arts as well as impassioned impact in the local political arena.

And then one day my friend **couldn't figure out why their passion had bottomed out**. And that moment—which they can distinctly describe—was the beginning of the end.

The end?! The end of what?!

Clasp your hands. How are you feeling about being a human? How do you think about being a human? How is the human-thing working for you in this timeplace that feels dangerous where the stream of environmental and sociopolitical data hasn't been trending "better" for some time, everywhere?

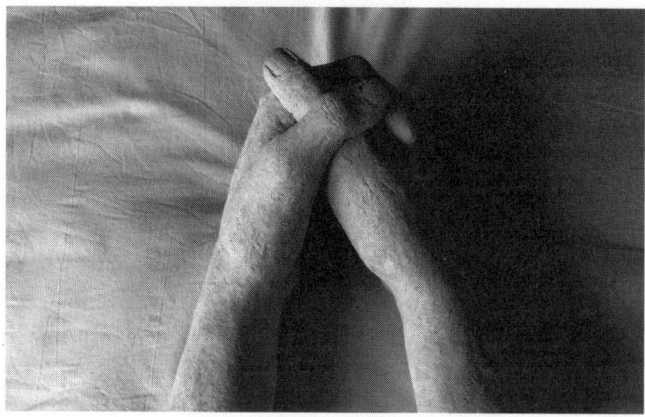

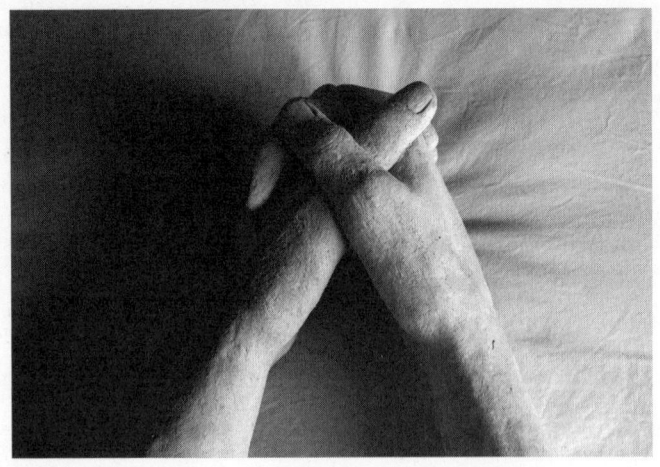

Clasp your hands. This isn't about prayer.
Or, maybe, it is.
Not.
Yes . . . useful to sigh.
And if we are to sigh
Make it count!
This thing we assume is our advantage
Over obstacles
In invention
And all life forms
Skittering about
As far as we are concerned
Our advantage over all beings
This thing
Called
Being
Human.
Invincibility assumed
Nobility transpired

Mastery fought for
Desire unrequited . . .
Clasp your hands. This isn't about prayer.
Or, maybe, it is.
Not.
Puzzling
Feeling
The hole of inadequacy
In this moment
The timeplace of collapse
Why isn't it working out
This thing
Called
Being human?
Perhaps the left hand
And the right hand
Haven't figured it out
Can't grasp the way
So worn the path of the human
Race
So worn.
Out
Of the shadows of persuasive doubt
Unbounded fear
Masking delusion
Suspicion rises
Like the tide
Some feel is rising
And some know
The land sinks
No matter

Both are so
The results the same
As it turns out
Like the tide.
Clasp your hands. This isn't about prayer.
Or, maybe, it is.
Not.
Some thing calls
Some thing stirs

If

And only if

We see what cannot be seen

And hear what cannot be heard

If
We examine this thing
What it means
What it can be
What it must become
This thing
Being Human.

CHAPTER 2

Don't Settle for What You Know

Whenever and wherever successful people meet a nether—which, by definition, is much more than a bump, a detour, or a dramatic pause—in their otherwise productive lives, there is a rupture. Sometimes the interruption is but a seed taking root in a bit of scrappy soil. Sometimes an unwelcome jokester makes comments in one's mind. Sometimes a growing cloud casts shade. Seeds grow roots. Jokesters are . . . annoying. Shades chill. And that may be the end of it, this condition we feel as a dampening of energy, perhaps thought of as a momentary lapse due to the fatigue of everyday life. But if the condition extends and grows like tropical mold, we enter the malaise of the nether.

Okay. Before we continue. I am neither a therapist nor behavioral scientist. Uh uh. None of that. If you're looking for that kind of advice and knowledge, you'll need to look elsewhere. I am not even the kind of writer who would look up the appropriate citations! Lazy in that respect, some would say. I say I'm not interested in building a body of work for people to believe in. Not my thing. And I fully, fully respect the authors who are laboring to provide heft of scholarship and understanding.

If neither therapist nor behavioral scientist, then what? I admit to being a deep observer of the human condition and our many-faceted characteristics, and the patterns of behaviors as they may play themselves out and intersect with human and natural events as they unfold. This started early in life, so much so that I have taken this small parcel of skill for granted, assuming even that everyone has it, for sure. Being physically clumsy and lacking good enough depth perception to know how far away a ball may be from my hand, face, shin, foot, or stomach, I mostly walked or ran by myself for a bit around the playground, then perched on the concrete stairs in the same peasant squat my Popo and Goong Goong used, waiting for fish to bite. A teacher came by and asked what I was looking at so intently. A fight is about to happen. Over there. And it did. This incident took place in the first or second grade, and so it has been.

No thing happens by itself. If this were a one-time thing, it would not even be worth remembering. In fact, I had forgotten about it, reminded only by a question recently asked, out of the blue. No thing happens by itself. While separated by activity and ability—my schoolmates played and I did not, my schoolmates could hit and catch balls and I not so much—I nonetheless felt deep connection and responsibility to all of my fellow little beings. (A fight is about to break out. Over there.) An island thing, perhaps, where community is just air, which allows for odd ducks to be a part of the ecosystem of useful beings. Later—much later—I would understand this to be an essential particle of indigeneity as it meets the multicultural environment of Hawai'i. Later—much later—there would be an absolute alignment of the ways Zen meditative and physical practices would enhance all the pathways of sensory observation and knowing.

There are innumerable incidents happening in anyone's life. We tend to think about accumulation as a linear trend. Your life got better and better and then everything fell apart. Or your life has always sucked and the good thing that happened once was just a good thing that happened once, and it wasn't that good anyway. The actual data, if we were able to minutely measure on some watch device without using said device to bio-adjust our experiences, would reveal a more nuanced and circular pathway. Our micro experiences form up as may a 3D pointillist painting, each incident a tiny dot of pure color that blends over millions of moments in our mind's eye, forming an overall impression of who we are, and what we are made of. Each incident is a sensory bundle in itself of sights and sounds and smells and feels, held together with thoughts, thoughts, thoughts. "It" happened, as in past tense, and yet a nano particle of the sensory bundle + thought embeds in one's cellular memory, reinforced by the next, edited by the next next, overtaken by the next next next.

Most of this, of course, is unconscious. Why? Because otherwise we would blow our minds. Just because we are not consciously aware does not mean "it" isn't happening, along with the accumulated impressions and impacts. It is environmental noise building up or stripping away, until you suddenly notice the din, or the absolute silence. Mostly without consciously knowing and occasionally noticing with wonder or alarm, we go about perceiving the world and making hundreds of decisions and actions each day, mostly in accordance with a predictable and patterned flight plan. We are the left-thumb-over-right-thumb people and it works. Or the right-thumb-over-left-thumb people and it works.

Until it doesn't.

Okay. Try this. If you are a left thumb over right thumber, try unclasping your hands in entirety and re-clasp them with right thumb over left thumb, making sure each interlacing finger has moved down a notch. (In other words, don't just change the thumbs. Come on. Do it. Actually. Not in your head.) And vice versa. How does that work for you? If you are like most folx, it will feel awkward, like this is not who you are and what you know. The awkwardness is a natural response, worthy of pause.

We are who we are. Deeply patterned. Informed by neurons and DNA and experiences and environment from the time we take our first breath and, some would say, even before we were born. Deeply patterned with defaults and well-worn muscles. Why would we buck that? Is it even possible? We are, after all, we are who we are. Well. Because it works until it doesn't. And then it would really suck if we just said oh well, we are who we are. That should bother you as an individual; if it doesn't, there is choice. But looking across the vast horizon of all humans as they may live in this precarious moment, it would really, really suck if everyone just said oh well, we are who we are.

There is choice. And we really, really need some people to choose. Right Now.

What are we choosing into? To move beyond what we are comfortable about and what it is we know. To stretch into what we don't yet know to evolve and become the humans these times and this earth requires of us. To choose not to settle for what we know. For the left-thumb-over-right-thumb people to embrace the part of them that has a right-thumb-over-left-thumb facet, and for the right-thumb-over-left-thumb people to understand the part of them that is also left-thumb-over-right-thumb. In other words, to bring as much of our whole selves as we can and can become to the current and future enterprise called being human on Mother Earth.

Wholeness does not mean sameness or symmetry. I am sure this will be spoken of more in future chapters. The little bit to grasp at this moment is to settle into the knowing that wholeness isn't about us having or achieving equality of strengths and tendencies.

Remember? Just trying it out by clasping and re-clasping shows you that to be both is an embodied improbability. Instead, we are seeking being more rounded-out, more filled-in, more multi-faceted and less habitually predictable, less rigidly compartmentalized, less one-legged in our standing.

The fact is we need the more expansive human to show up these days, and the danger and stress of the times also create a crosswind driving us back into the shells of what we know and believe we can rely upon, the tried-and-true formulae of who we are. "The definition of insanity is doing the same thing over and over again and expecting different results," Albert Einstein did not say. Seriously. It is a saying attributed to Einstein and we believe it because it sounds like something the scientist-inventor-provocateur would say, but there is no evidence that he said it or wrote it. It nonetheless encapsulates where we are as a human race. We cannot rely on the tried-and-true formulae and do the same thing over and over again, expecting somehow for more effort or more belief in effort to transport us beyond the human-induced mess of current circumstances. No more than saying over and over again that Albert Einstein said something would make it true.

Don't settle for what you know! Even in who it is we are. This is the simple antidote to the malaise of the nether.

Time and time again, applying the known rules to situations the rules were not made for will merely frustrate us. Recently, the Social Security Administration took steps to remove out-of-date occupations from the list used to see if someone would be able to claim disability. Surely you are not completely disabled if you can still sort nuts? Operate a pneumatic tube? Learn how to be a banking pin adjuster? The rules are the rules.

We tend to accept rules—whether we like them or not, believe them to be sensical or not—as fixed boundaries in narrow pathways.

If they show up in this way, it is because they are often purposely constructed in restrictive, prescriptive, and/or circumscribed ways. This I observe, neutral to content. Every worthy rule writer will aim toward a level of specificity that takes many things into consideration to close as many loopholes as possible against the flaunting of rules by the reluctant, the lazy, the naysayer, the chronic rule breaker, the procrastinator, the cunning, the righteous, and the forgetful. (You are, of course, none of these.) Though rules are merely the implementation dos and don'ts of broader intentions, we remarkably forget those intentions once we are fixated on the solid lines of rules. No dotted lines, no passing allowed. No stopping allowed.

Thus, we would find ourselves in the year 2024 rather sheepishly admitting that the list of unskilled sedentary jobs that certainly would be in reach of anyone before they are deemed to be so disabled they will qualify as disabled, perhaps this list should not include becoming a nut sorter, as nut sorters are no longer in much demand in the United States. (What is a nut sorter?!)

To work through the reasoning would require us to zoom out of the detail and focus instead on intent. And intent brings us into an uneasy realm of human understanding: our understanding of and fidelity to reasons, motivations, and hopeful impacts. We are more comfortable with the specificity of rules, whether or not we agree with said rules, such that we will litigate and change the rules even when the intent no longer serves us instead of arguing the intent no longer applies and therefore no number of changing rules will free us from the yoke. Our minds are trapped in the place of believing all we need are better rules. No, no, no.

We most certainly need more than the rule maker and the rule keeper and the rule breaker to show up these days! To think and believe these three encompass the entirety of human possibilities is an exercise of inevitability as we cling to the comfort of what it is we know. Recognize the well-worn tendency, the habit pattern, and break free. Don't settle for what you know. The human species has been around for about two hundred thousand years (for those who believe anthropological evidence). That is about ten thousand generations. If our ancestral humans held tight to the comfort of what it is they knew, I certainly wouldn't be typing these words and you wouldn't be reading them, among many other phenomena of remarkable changes over the ten thousand generations. I readily admit to the remarkable number of less than useful, less than wise changes in the thinking and at the hands of our collective human ancestors. Still, faced with the peril and the angst, the danger and the sorrow of this rapidly unfolding time, surely, we would grasp the generational imperative to **not** settle for what we know.

CHAPTER 3

The Human Quotient (H_u)

In my slim *When No Thing Works*, there is a tiny chapter on H_u. This book is about that chapter.

Who we are matters. Much focus is given to what it is we do, and what it is we have. The being part counts at least as much, if not more. Being is the *je ne sais quoi*, the X factor. While irreplaceable, it is renewable. Being is more essential energy than a solid object, though nothing substantive is possible without beings showing up. Who are we **be**ing? And who are we **be**coming? A being is most evident in the timeplace of consciousness. In unconscious existence, we are closer to living machines than living beings, capable of reflexive and formulaic thoughts and actions but not so much in the realm of surprise, creativity, complex decision-making. There is an aliveness to beingness that cannot be denied or easily hidden. A great actor is being a character in their entirety—spirit, physicality, past, present, and future—so much so that the actor disappears and has become the character they stepped into. The mere craft of acting is insufficient for beingness. To act implies artifice. We can tell when someone is trying too hard to be someone they are clearly not, at least not yet. Beingness emanates from some inner space of knowing. It is genuine and true. A baby is. A grown-up may retreat into some other skin or uniform, finding their way back when there is nothing more to prove.

Who we are matters. The beingness part is a significant part of the Human Quotient. And there is character. Some believe that we are born rather neutral, not knowing or caring that the cereal we grab from our sister's tray belongs to her and therefore it is a taking. Most eventually learn what is right and what is wrong. We learn the behaviors admired and scorned by the people we are attached to and the pods we are a part of. Psychology is not my thing, so there will be no opining on how a person may stray away from behavioral characteristics evident in people who are close to them or change radically after a seminal event in their lives. It happens. Some characteristics appear very close to birth, so are unlikely to have been learned from other beings or from environmental conditioning. Courage appears very early in life, as does inquisitiveness, as well as the lack thereof. And that characteristic called introvert, extrovert, or ambivert appears to be baked into the behavioral personality of who we are well before we are out of our twos and threes.

In the Human Quotient needed to take the productive leap when the juncture arrives where change is possible and therefore begins, there are a handful of essential characteristics.

Courage is very near the top of the list. Without courage, no big leaps can be made. Period. Leaps require risk-taking. Without risk, there can be no big change, significant pivot, dramatic expansion of our understanding. And risk is very difficult to hold and navigate for the faint of heart, or the fool who doesn't understand or perhaps care about impacts and dangers. Which is to say a person who is blind to peril imperils others and is, therefore, not a courageous person at all. Within the bundled core of courage is the willingness to face defeat and victory equally without hesitation. Courage comes in many packages: quiet, fierce, leading, following, for and with, seen and unseen.

Further ahead on the list is a characteristic that is less succinct to describe than "courage," the element of the Human Quotient that depends on our capacity and willingness to come from and lean into our own humanity, and the humanity of and with others, including nonhuman beings and those humans who are determined to evolve toward their worse selves. Without the characteristic, the value, the compass, the capacity to build more muscle for our shared humanity, our future as a species is . . . bleak. The quote "Hurt people hurt people" has been used so often it is singularly unattributable. Given all the hurt rained down over the eons and accelerating in the near present, hurt refusing to be reined in, there is no doubt there are a preponderance of hurt people in the world. It is much too simple to say we should expect, therefore, for there to be just hurt people hurting other people for the remainder of our species' existence. The notion of no agency is antithetical to human experience. In the most horrific of circumstances—slavery, imprisonment, genocide, disenfranchisement—a cup of water is offered, a smile shared, beauty found, love blooms even in grief, immense unheralded sacrifices made for the sake of others, among innumerable small acts of humanity. That there is still slavery, imprisonment, genocide, disenfranchisement, and many other horrific acts by individuals, institutions, and nation-states speaks to the many ways we have devalued our connection and kuleana (mutual responsibility) to and with other human beings. Our humanity quotient is indeed at a sore and slippery nadir where consciousness is viewed by too many as a weakness. We may call upon the "Hurt people hurt people" adage to describe the why. A lazy way out, I say with an admission of judgment. Too many times, humanity is bypassed by the privileged and the privileged part within us. We can deny, we can hurt, and gain power or a following or elation or inflation of ego and worthiness by these thoughts and actions, and so we do.

What's more, we don't care. This last part is how you know humanity has left the house called this person who doesn't care, at least for the foreseeable future. Humanity does not require perfection. It **does** require evolution, which may very well require the fiercest resistance to devolution until our muscles are realigned to the ways of creation rather than destruction.

Our humanity must be evolving toward our better selves in order to be compassionate. Compassion by itself—without courage, just a set piece standing in for humanity, sans wisdom—works in overdrive pulling the struggling folx out of the fast-moving stream, without the capacity or understanding to keep folx from falling in to begin with. As a driver onto itself, compassion can have unintended consequences requiring cleanup in aisle five. A skewing toward charity in which things are done by some group for another group, building dependency. A lack of discernment placing a burden on those who were intended to be helped, as occurred when tens of thousands of well-meaning Northern Hemisphere folx sent unneeded blankets and turtlenecks and sweaters to Southern Hemisphere folx during the December 2004 Indian Ocean earthquake and tsunami. (When it is cold in the north it is generally warm and humid in the south. Happens every year. It is science.)

To be clear, natural and human-induced disasters are plentiful. We have endless opportunities to practice compassion and it is very important to remain open in our thinking and feelings for other human beings, to be of support when we can. Endless opportunities can become background noise. That we see, hear, and respond is important. How we respond also matters. In the immediate hours and days after the August 2023 fires at Lahaina, Maui, the west side of the island was practically cut off from the less impacted east side. In the days and weeks to follow, tens of thousands of people from the islands and beyond carried out many acts of giving, caring, service, and kindness. Countless. But the fires were not yet fully extinguished when the first to come to the aid were folx from Molokaʻi, an island of simple living with high unemployment about eight miles away, arriving by small boats with whatever it is they had in their closets, garages, and freezers. Their aloha will never be forgotten.

My teacher spent several years in conversations with Native Hawaiian elders Pilahi Paki and Nana Veary, honing his understanding of aloha. Compassion is a critical Buddhist precept, but difficult to penetrate. Tanouye Roshi understood aloha as the manifestation of wise compassion. Understand and live aloha, and we will be the wisely compassionate people we hope to be. Aloha is held in mutuality in which "each person is important to every other person for collective existence." This last part is in quotes because it is directly stated in a Hawaiʻi state law, so important to our understanding of who we are and, therefore, our obligations to each other. "Aloha means to hear what is not said, to see what cannot be seen and to know the unknowable," the law continues. This is directly from guidance left by Liliʻuokalani, the last leader of the Native Hawaiian people before the government overturned and lands seized. Even in unspeakable loss and an uncertain future, we are required by aloha to have the discernment that arises because of our essential connectivity to humans, other beings, and the earth. If we lose that then we have lost more than our rights of self-governance. This robust, spirit-filled aloha was Tanouye Roshi's brand of compassion. "Aloha is water. Its strength can overcome everything, and yet it flows to the place of least resistance. It is life itself," he said. It is life. The aloha of the people of Molokaʻi for the people of Maui and Maui for Molokaʻi will never be forgotten.

Intelligence isn't required for compassion, but wisdom is. Or at least a trend line toward wisdom. Wisdom is definitely in the top five essential characteristics needed to take the productive leap when the juncture arrives where change is possible and therefore begins. In this timeplace in which information is aggregated and quickly disseminated, there is an accumulation of knowledge by many. Knowledge is not the same as wisdom. No matter how many Wikipedia pages you read, strung together from keyword to subject, will make you a wiser person. You may be more knowledgeable, achieve contestant status on *Jeopardy*, or win trivia night at the local bar, but **to be wise** is a different state of being than knowing all things. It cannot arise as a matter of accumulation of the detritus of social media feeds. Within wisdom is good judgment that does not judge, good choices understanding the gravity of choices, good humility to accompany the kuleana of being a person who is counted on to be wise.

H$_u$—the Human Quotient—is an essential element, with more elastic qualities than any element on the periodic table. Who we are matters a lot in our individual lives, and even more on a collective basis. The question of whether we can count on our collective humanity is not just for morose philosophers nursing whiskey neats! Indeed, illuminating this essential element is a hopeful question for all of us. Why? Because, as humans, we can do something about ourselves. We can change, hone, interrupt, leap, shed, get off our you-know-what, be more courageous, summon wisdom, practice aloha. We can arise.

CHAPTER 4

Will We Choose Humanity?

Alarmingly so, we—the current descendants of the human race—are not. That we are unable to see our choices as **self**-destruction is a mystery.

Instead of humanity, we choose "othering," defined in the *Oxford* online dictionary as "viewing or treating a person or a group of people as intrinsically different and alien to oneself." Othering is our go-to. They don't understand. They are terrible. They think they're better than us. If not for them, we would be winning, be better off, get what we want. Othering is very, very self-centered. It depends on the armoring of perfection of who we are in juxtaposition to others, though paradoxically rendering us curiously thin-skinned to any criticism. We take offense in defense of ourselves, and our point of view. Othering is an equal ideological partner. It occurs equally on the left as it does on the right, to the extreme left as it does to the left, to the left of center to the center, to the right of center to the right, to the extreme right. Have all the bases been covered? If you can be labeled, if you can label, you can other. If you reject labels, you can other those who label and vice versa. Othering is much more efficient in keeping us apart than cornstarch or flour or wax paper or parchment paper or fancy-pants silicone pads. It preserves an illusion of fault assignment. We are never responsible for anything bad that happens. Successes are our own. Othering stirs all of our emotive juices, but especially those along the anger to hatred spectrum. Othering is righteous and has no doubts.

To be clear, there are many ways othering can be justified. I have very specific thoughts and feelings about the waves of people who brought disease to these islands, assumed property ownership, gifted goats, assumed the superiority of English, polluted. I have enough details to know about these things as specific events as well as aggregate behaviors, as the near inevitable results of the beliefs and ambitions of countries as well as the desires of individuals. Plus greed, indifference, and lots of othering. Even love between my ancestors can be narrated in othering. The Chinese contract workers found much more in common with the native people than the white owners and managers who were, for the most part, citizens of a country that excluded people of Asian lineage from naturalizing and often came from places prohibiting white and Asian marriages. The partnering of Native Hawaiian and Chinese was common, a product of affinity as well as a product of common othering.

My story is common for this place. Many stories are common in many places, frequently narrated along fault lines of race, hues, class, gender, and ability. That othering is universally found does not mean it needs to be so.

To choose ways of being that are beyond othering requires choosing to reconnect the parts of us that were once whole, more open, less discriminating. Before we learned things, absorbed things, made sense of things on the streets or in books, the IGs, or screeds. Before we became accustomed to making decisions quickly based on the barest of impressions, the telltale signs of identity or behaviors or language or appearance that would categorize people in the containers of otherness. It feels like a long, long time ago in an innocent and naive past.

Okay. Let us park that thought for a bit and ask the question: why bother?

Trusting the truly cynical wouldn't even pick up this book, let's address the spectrum from very discouraged to somewhat doubtful.

Othering, and its mirror twin called "speaking to the choir," is a strategy to reinforce a core base of like-minded people. It will feel like a group is becoming larger and stronger because each effort awakens, enlivens, energizes, and gathers the like-minded in relationship with each other. So far, we, the like-minded, haven't increased in numbers. We have found each other and are no longer isolated individuals believing we are alone. When you are not alone, it will feel like growth, though mathematically speaking, 1 + 1 + 1 + 1 + 1 = 5, whether the "ones" are spread out randomly in a stadium filled with people not knowing of each other's existence, or huddled together in front of a concession stand, realizing we all wore the same shirt with the same slogan. Part of us may believe we are the only ones; after all, what are the odds? And part of us will absolutely believe there are more and begin to search us out. Whether we are five of the forty thousand, or four thousand of the thirty-two million, mathematically speaking we are the same number to begin with as individuals as we may be aggregated. Of course, something does happen together rather than apart from. Together we are emboldened, appreciated, and group permissioned. Energy is created in the air between us, and ideas emerge. Our individual selves are magnified. Even so, the math remains math, and speaking to the choir, the mirror twin of othering, will not in and of itself create "more."

This math problem is exacerbated by splintering, a natural feature of othering. Othering has a way of becoming more and more defined with litmus tests, precise categories, fealty, and betrayal. From the outside, it may all look like ambitious bickering. Inside, there is a constant proving into the group's identity. From the outside, we may be dismayed or entertained by the public name-calling between US Representative Lauren Boebert and US Representative Marjorie Taylor Greene. From the outside, the distinctions between "rights," "reform," and "justice" seem academic, definitions with little distinction. Inside, the fight to hyper-represent is tangible. So-called political correctness, used these days as an epithet from the right to the left, is a sought and rejected behavior across the spectrum. That the distinctions and subsequent fight-fault lines are difficult to keep up with, so quickly they might shape-shift, is part of the phenomenon of splintering into smaller and smaller groups. Splintering multiplies and subtracts at the same time. Splintering means more groups (which is the multiplication part) and smaller wholes (that's the subtraction part).

It is very difficult to construct an enduring, successful large-scale strategy for any set of ideas based on othering, splintering, and the denial of the humanity of those we are othering. Math alone works against such a plan, especially in places requiring some formulation of majority or plurality. Even in places where absolute and punishing power is both strategy and reward, it is difficult to permanently deny the ambition of aspiring despots or to compel large numbers of people to work against their own interests day in and day out. Such societies become smaller, more isolated, less creative, not as productive, all the while exacting an unbearable human toll. And yet, each day's news shows us the many ways we can define our possibilities by denying the desires, needs, and the very lives of other people. We choose ourselves, as we may narrowly define the "our" and the "self." It is not a winning choice.

So. Taking a deep breath here. Will we choose humanity? If we, the human race, are to have a chance at making the turn toward increasing prospects, better health, shorter conflicts, productive and satisfying lives, we do indeed need to make the choice. Released from tepid acceptance, the times call for letting go of our justified and righteous notions of how others are responsible for the less than desirable conditions of this timeplace and taking responsibility for how we extract ourselves with the most expansive notion of "we" and "our" as we can muster. There is little time to twiddle! We are indeed in that tight timeplace approaching a nether. Some would even say that we have passed into the event horizon[1] from which it would be extraordinarily difficult to reverse the decline and chaos. It is true. This will require extraordinary effort, a collective focusing on choosing into humanity.

CHAPTER 5

We Are the Ancestors of Descendants Yet to Come

We are the ancestors of descendants yet to come.
Even I
A woman of few attachments
With no children
Even I
Am an ancestor of descendants yet to come
Just as the ancient stars are ancestors
Of every atom of every being
Across the vastness of timespace
Looking up into Elder Sky
Cloud, Abode of God

空
Esibhakabhakeni
Lani
The heavens vast
Not The Heaven Beyond
Indeed a part of
Who it is we were

And yet still becoming
This our ancestors wondered
As they wandered
So far and so long
They forgot
Who they originally were
And where they originally lived
So long ago the memory could not be held
One song to another
Story
Chant
Scratched on bamboo strips
And weathered away on rock
Ten thousand generations
A rope too long
To be held by humans and yet
The night sky held it all
As we peered into the vault
Holding the secrets of our birth
The calcium in our bones
The iron of our blood
Our muscles' carbon
Knitting nucleotides in our DNA
Just stardust
Born of profound darkness
For longer than all humankind
And brightness as unborn stars died
Exploding across the
Elder Sky
Cloud, Abode of God

空

Esibhakabhakeni
Lani
The heavens vast
Not The Heaven Beyond
Indeed in every atom of who it is we were and will always be
A part of
Not separate from
All beings and indeed
Mother Earth
Herself a repository of
Who it is we were
And are
And will be
The ancestors of descendants yet to come
The untold
The yet to be sung
Beings
Remembering what it is we are
As we were
Before the time of forgetting
The place of displacement
Before we saw night just as that time
When lights are turned on
To keep the day's brightness longer
And crowd the dark silence
Forcing a pause
In the maelstrom of things
We have become accustomed to
The many things

To covet and hold and admire and keep and discard
For other things
To covet and hold and admire and keep and discard
The many things
Keeping company
With the many voices, sounds, words
Fed in chips, audiofiled, opined
By influencers and bloggers
The loudest-among-us
All day long
And into the night held back
All day long
Lights turned on
Juiced to be what it is we believe it is to be alive
We the ancestors of descendants yet to be
Held back the tide of our own understanding
As long as we could
As we ran the clock
Of human invention
Of all the things and ways
We ran and ran until we could not run
Away from who it is we are
Each in a lane of our own making
Not knowing not caring
Others
Running too
Away from without knowing the to
No future in mind
Only
The me and mine
Not the you and yours

Mostly the not that
Just this
Everyone has something to say
Sez me
All day long
On repeat
So it seemed
In a one sudden moment
Or at least it seemed
A sudden moment in which
We
The human race
Burst through our own skins just
As the ancient unborn stars died
So did we
We
Stopped.

For a long while
There was profound
Profound darkness
Though the world kept moving on
We did not
As if timeplace disappeared
And nothing existed beyond
The oxygen in our lungs
Carbon muscles
Bones, calcium
Iron in our blood
Red born of
Oxygen in our lungs!

Finally manifest
Just because
We paused long enough
To notice
Profound darkness
Though the world kept moving on
As it always has been in the shortness of our one life
As it always has been
And yet
In the darkness the potent question arose
Is this so
And must it be
The potent question arose
Before there is light
There must be the many Pō^2
Not just
The one
Flat
Dark
Without dimension
No hope
No breath
Born of
Oxygen in our lungs
As exists and gifted
From ancient stars
We can now see
Their light
Hurtling toward us
In the night sky
Our heads up

Not glued to screens and screeds
Our heads up
Wondering
Again
As we are intended to
This one human trait
Of wonder
Making our way
A wander
Toward the barest of light
Breathing life
And pulsing
Even, it seems
There is life in this light
And we do not yet know
Though we wonder
If this light pulses within us
Or without
A creature
A being of its own
As all scattering
Of supernovae may be
Perhaps the ancient part of us
Is showing a new way
Or at least
It seems
It feels
It is becoming
Something new
Too old to have a name
In the beginning

Once again
An unborn becoming
May we pause
Long enough to
Hold in wonder
Not deceit
We have the receipts
How can we not
Having finally come out of the long slumber
Born of franticness
Set aside
For
Oxygen in lungs
A novelty somehow
After all of this time
We still know
How to breathe
Again
As we sit
As still as we may
Having lost that muscle
Of wonder
Having wandered too fast and too far
Away
From our own piko
Our bellybutton
Reminding us
We too were just recently connected
To an ancestor
And they to them
Piko a piko

We now sit
As still as we may
Listening to the
Night sky within
Us the pulsing being
Of whom we are becoming
Please
May it be
The many ancestors
Of descendants yet to come
Once more
Seeing what cannot be seen
Hearing what cannot be heard
Examining this thing
What it means
What it can be
What it must become
This thing
Being Human.

CHAPTER 6

The Opposite of War Is Creation

In the Broadway show *Rent*, American composer and playwright Jonathan Larson wrote, "The opposite of war isn't peace . . . It's creation!" Bravo, Jonathan Larson.

In war, whether carried out through military means or not, there will be violence. Violence deployed in opposition to violence is an expected high conflict that can sometimes but not always, and some would argue only rarely will, result in one side winning in totality, resulting in the other side losing in entirety. The cessation of violence does not mean there is or will be peace. And peace, in itself, is an insufficient state of affairs to prevent violence and war. The engagement and the cessation of war, war and peace, aren't mutually exclusive.

Peace as it may be held as a null state, a void, an absence of, can easily collapse upon itself. A vibrant growing well-being in a society willing to productively struggle with all of the scary and unknown things toward wholeness of all beings in relationship to each other is an energetic waging of peace. It is creation.

And creation is uniquely human.

Okay, okay. The aspirants of AI will surely disagree. That AI can replicate human aspiration is an unfortunate data point . . . with an emphasis on *replication*. Which is to say that when we—the humans—are iterative in our thinking, lazily cut and paste, cease to inspire and be inspired, reflexively act, draw upon the tried-and-true strategies for the hundredth time, rinse and repeat, we are settling for the human equivalents of AI. Ouch.

True story. This morning my sister texted me as she lazed for a bit in the wee hours before preparing for work, she in the bedroom and me in the living room, about fifty feet apart. Just the easy banter of one old sister to another old sister, with a bit of text teasing as I receive and send from an old model flip phone, where "999 pause 33 pause 7777" = "yes." "Emphasizing you need a SMART PHONE," texted she, emphasis included. "Because I like stay smart is why no moa smart phone," texted me. (Read "no moa" as "no more.")

There are all kinds of ways modernity interferes with our innate creativity, siphoning the juices we were born with. We are born as curious beings, peering into the world with wonder, inserting as many of our own stories into the mix of things as we may learn so-called data, facts, proper names, constructs of why. As young ones we sensually experience, absorb, imagine, colorfully manifest in our mind's eye, with fewer if any of the constraints, judgment, and reticence that come with our adult mind-body forms. What we are called to do or required to do as an adult may remove the joy or the need or time or means or energy for regular and even periodic creative expression. And there are all the constructions of modernity. Dating myself, as a young policy planner at my first American Planning Association meeting, I took careful note of a speaker extolling the ways the desktop would revolutionize planning. Less than ten years later, the same speaker brought a flip chart and handful of markers on the stage, warning against the ease of cut and paste and the absence of rigor when it is too easy to produce a pretty package. The devices, the software, the apps, the vast search engines are tools, just as are the flip chart, the Post-its, the Mr. Sketch nontoxic markers. Some tools make it easier to imaginatively explore. And some tools are designed to pre-fill and need to be taken off auto or just set aside from time to time or weaned away from.

Modernity and the devices of modernity can also fill every moment of every day with addictive buzz and yada yada, memes, YouTubes, influencer endorsements, and ads about ads. We follow and are followed, are voyeurs and exhibitionists. The mobility and ubiquity of devices means we have access to and can be accessed, filling every moment of every day such that rules and laws have to be passed to keep us nominally safe from being unaware in a moving vehicle we are supposedly operating, or being unaware of crossing a street.

Being entertained can respond to and satiate our imagination but rarely creates the conditions for our own creation.

Imagination and creation require spaciousness.

Spaciousness is actual space! A canvas, a blank sheet of paper, a nook, an empty table waiting to be filled with deliciousness of our own making. Spaciousness is time. More than just a few minutes crammed in here and there. The luxuriousness versus luxury of a morning to one's own wandering and musing. Spaciousness is a mind free of clutter and looping worries and the competition of this and that. Spaciousness sits in mostly quiet, that we may actually hear and experience the sounds around us. Spaciousness is a useful empty cup.

Spaciousness is a necessary condition to cultivate wonderment, the stuff of creation. Wonderment is the awe of life, the human capacity to appreciate without the embellishment of judgment. It emanates from curiosity, though less an inhabitant of the Socratic mind and more a wondrous sigh ending in a happy exclamation point. As a thinker, I can endlessly wonder, otherwise known as wandering wonder. But no thing worthy of sharing with myself or others will arise in the noise of my own mind. The humble jewels emerge as dawn makes itself known and incubate in the night sky.

Without wonderment I am unable to imagine the mechanisms of an interdependent world in which each person is important to every other person for collective existence, to create into the many things and conditions of this kind of world. Creation starts in the spaciousness of our imagination and moves quickly into the narrating story, the design, the gathering of people and things, the birthing and building, the cultivation, pruning, and harvesting. Rinse and repeat. Creation is an imperative, as words and ideas and slogans and dreams are scant defenses in a collapsing world wearily accepting the inevitability of violence and war.

In order for there to be the kind of durable peace that honestly and bravely meets the timespace when no thing works, evolution is the directionality of our creation. Evolution accepts the data of what is and leans into what will be and what we choose to become. If we the ancestors of descendants yet to come are to embrace the kuleana, the sacred and mutual responsibility, of our role in this timespace, then the conscious evolution of the human race is ours to create.

CHAPTER 7

Big Leaps

=

Strategy$^{\text{Human Quotient}}$

To be clear, the collectively accelerating timespace requires us to take **Big Leaps**. There is a Human Quotient aspect to this, and a strategy component, with the relationship between the two described in the formula that is the title of this chapter. A big leap manifests in a strategy that is only as good as the core characteristics, behaviors, and fealty to humanity of the people who are creating, holding, implementing, and leaning into the strategy. In mathematics, the superscript is an exponent, and in that parlance describes the value of the exponential power. Such is the intention here. The Human Quotient exponentially raises the potential, the power, the energy, the efficacy, the bigness of a strategy and, therefore, the quality and bigness of a leap. If you do not pay attention to the nature of the Human Quotient, then your strategy, no matter how cleverly crafted, will have an exponent no greater than the power of 1.

It is useful to explore this equation in more than the typical leaderly constructs. In the big leaps required to shift the course of humankind and reverse the cycle of destruction, individual leadership is insufficient. An equation dependent on leadership would have too long of a lag time between need/opportunity and implementation, and too large of a differential between extent of effort required and alignment among all the individually led entities. This is as much about the construct of modern leadership as anything else, and the ways in which we both depend upon the levers of leadership to determine things while lagging behind in the human endeavoring of execution. Typical leaderly constructs have built-in limitations. Instead of the equation above, leadership offers drag coefficients fencing in and qualifying the bigness of leaps. It is important, for example, to understand the importance of courage in people writ large, rather than focusing on whether a leader is courageous or not. Our dependence and reliance on individual leadership is a human infrastructure fault line. Just like natural fault lines, catastrophic phenomena will shake up and weaken the thin line of individual leadership, and all in their wake will be vulnerably unsettled as well. In a leaderly construct, we pick leaders as best we can, then shore them up as both the core and front line of our aspirations, needs, offense, and defense. In a Human Quotient way of understanding, leaders are decision-makers in strategies to cultivate the collective human potential. Who decisions are made by may change depending on who has the experience and characteristics we, the community, require. Wherever and whenever there are more people than not who are courageous, clear-eyed, wise, energetic, coming from and moving toward aloha, wherever and whenever this is the case then bigger leaps will occur, more ground covered, breakthroughs abound in nearly effortless ways because effort is generated in excited willingness from many.

A strategy is only as good as the people who are executing it. All strategies must ask the many "who" questions: who will lead, who will manage, who will be the many implementors, who will benefit, who will lose, who will support, who will detract, who will oppose, who will care, and who will not care. More than asking, the answers of the who and the characteristics of the who should inform and shape the strategy. Any strategy that doesn't take the people part of it with due seriousness will underperform if not fail. Strategies are not interchangeable between peoples, places, circumstances, and the interlaced relationships between peoples, places, circumstances.

Strategies are needed for big leaps. Big leaps are not just a matter of leaders or groups of people (or even really large groups of people) just leaping. The phenomenon of just leaping can happen with some regularity without it becoming a durable leap that shifts things. Especially in the desire for this to be a long moment of pivoting and creating the conditions and circumstances for healthier, happier, thriving enoughness, strategies are required. In the leap itself, there will be a period of time in which a part of who/what is leaping will leave the safety and comfort of the ground. Therefore, at the very least, we need to have a plan for how long/far we leave the ground, where/how we land, and where/how we move on from the new "here." If not, a leap can set you back, as did an unfortunate number of tragic Arab Springs.

A leap is not experienced as an iterative thing when it happens though there are iterative steps prior to leaping. We prepare ourselves. We practice. We make the decisions of when, where, and with whom. Significantly, there may be a period of processing in which we ask various iterations of the question of why, and in an overly long manner contemplate and hesitate, suspiciously reject and overly share. "Why?" is an extremely important question. How we go about answering it says a great deal about whether the leap will be big or not and what its success will be in the scheme of things. Questions of why are always central to the Human Quotient. In both strategy and human transformation, the central question is always "Why am I here?" The Why Question is The Question, the answer to which will unlock everything else yet to be determined. Without answering The Why, our actions are rudderless. "Why am I here?" is existential and, therefore, central to our humanity. Some will call this the "purpose" question, though I urge you to just set the label aside if the "p" word creates a barrier.

When there are more than a few people committed to a big leap and they do so, it will not seem like a leap to them though other folx will observe it as startling phenomena. It will not seem like a leap to them because it will simply be experienced as fluid movement, a simple arising up from the crouch or sit into a purposeful stride, skip, run for those who can. For those who are otherwise standing still or prone upon the ground, this movement all around them will seem like a leap. This difference in perception is a difference between observation and participation. How quickly the fish swim beyond our reach, say the humans standing and watching from the comfort of the rocks above, while the fish are not swimming beyond wherever they are swimming as far as the fish are concerned.

Human Quotient strategy requires observation and participation to be occurring at the same time. (Here I am tempted to insert a layperson's understanding of a physics discourse on spacelike and timelike separation . . . but I digress.) It is a natural thing to specialize in the parts of work we have affinity for, which frequently means it is work we are both good at and believe will render the most benefits. The bothness of endeavors isn't where we normally live, and in ordinary times, isn't required.

I labored, mostly productively, for nearly twenty-five years in the fields of political change, with a significant emphasis on the policy heft of things. To this day, my brain still works in the constructs of policy. Seeing and interrogating problems, following the thread of knots or unraveling as close to the source as may be possible, and doodling the connective web of decisions and actions that may shift conditions and outcomes. I think in mind maps and, for most of the early part of my life, believed that all I had to do was convince people who have agency to utilize this or another mind map for the benefit of the people we mutually cared about and the place that is our home. I am, after all, a right-thumb-over-left-thumb person. Of course, I knew that everyone didn't see a problem as I saw, nor did they necessarily desire the outcomes I sought. They may even desire that which I endeavored to change, in which case they would oppose change and strategies were required to overcome, convince, accommodate, or otherwise go around. I didn't think of it this way, but I guess you could have called me a systems-change kind of person. (With a side gig as a Zen student.)

It took a while, nearly twenty-five years, for the data to accumulate over innumerable scraps, projects, campaigns, successes, and failures to fully appreciate the cul-de-sac of systems change. Building, changing, working around, shifting, erecting alternatives, even factoring in the Human Quotient into systems-change strategies did little to spark meaningful human evolution. And unless we, the current members of that special club called the human race, unless we harness all of that privilege and step into the responsibilities of more than just our own success, we will be among the last of the descendants fighting over the structures at the end of a cul-de-sac. This I had to embrace with both right thumb over left thumb as well as left thumb over right thumb.

Change is improbable without leaping. No leap possible without strategy. No strategy available without human evolution. Let us begin.

CHAPTER 8

Wholeness Is Not Accommodation

Wholeness
As a slogan
Excellent for food

Including the spiritual kind
And as in food
More useful as food than slogan

To be
One With
Is wholeness

And wholeness
Just
Is

Wholeness
Is not accommodation
Of our troubled existence

Seeking to include
The farthest of one side
With the farthest of the other

Sides
All loud voices
Does not intactness make

Intactness is
Wholeness
Worthy of endeavor

Not accommodation
Not opposite of
Separation
Division
Subtraction of human life

Not accommodation
Not opposite of
Turmoil

As if a static state
Like a stale pond of
Politeness

Holding one's nose
Shutting tight the sounds
Of unfiltered diatribes

You know
Pretending
The kind we are capable of

Having come this far
Exceeding 144 characters
Can't ever be the whole of who we are

Becoming
Or even
Left behind

Our notion of
What is whole
And what is not

Just remove the "w"
And we clearly know
The hole

In the middle of our heart
Where grief used to productively water
Our loss

Giving way
To resolve's hard-fought hope
This hole we know

Ours to know and fill
From the darkness of Pō
To red dawn awakening

Our kuleana sacred
Mutual
Responsibility

In this endeavor
To know wholeness
Not as purity

How can it be
Static
Devoid of dirt and stain

Only the equity of sweat
Hard work
Will bring us safely to the other side

The other side
Beyond turmoil
Separation
Erasure

Yes, sanctity
But not righteous purity
As much hard work needs to be done

People fed
Streams, cooled and cleaned
Everything in between interrupted

For we do not yet really know
Wholeness
In this fully embraced way

Being
Neither on top nor bottom
This side or that

Replacing them with us
Will not the we make

We the ancestors of descendants yet to come
Reaching farther back than memory's dreams

Embracing
Original not knowing
In making this leap

We create the event horizon of the whole
Much more than accommodation
Don't you think?

No, don't think!
Instead adopt
Chuang Tzu's advice[3]

To listen with our spirit as the
Way gathers in this nether space
Emptied of our ambition

And all the things
All the noise
Giving way

To just a whisper
An earnest wind reminds the land
How whole all can be

In the multitude
Of life learning to be
One With

One peace at a time
One by One by One
Making our way

Figuring out Our
Figuring out Way
Figuring out what makes the whole whole

A fierce aloha
This enduring wind
Wholeness

CHAPTER 9

Evolution

Without evolution, revolution is a leap without strategy.

Revolutions and rebellions happen more frequently than one may think across recorded history to the present. A quick scan of the Wikipedia page is sobering. Just scan. Notice we have a reflexive judgment of whether a particular uprising was "good" or "bad" or "What was that about, anyway?" or "No, that wasn't, couldn't have been" or "It isn't on the list; no one noticed." Notice that violence is so common in revolts that the word "nonviolent" qualifies the rarely occurring nonviolent revolution.

A revolution is "a forcible overthrow of a government or social order in favor of a new system," according to the *Oxford* online dictionary. Whether an actual conversion occurs, rather than just the overthrow, hinges on how successful the successors are in **implementing** a new system. Too many times, faltering governments and social systems are toppled only to be replaced by the less competent or more brutal. Tragically, violence begets violence. More frequently than not, there is a long fallow period of no governance. Folx were so intent on the fight they gave meager thought and organizing to the steps thereafter. Equally terrible are the near misses when rebellions occur but fade, dissolve, or are pushed down without serious reckoning of the reasons for the arising, sowing the seeds for untended rot and discontent.

Revolutions and rebellions are societal-scale disrupters. Sticking the landing is critical to whether the disruption will bring about the betterment of the lives tossed at the sacrifice of the lost. There is the strategy part, the execution part, and the toward-what-end part. It cannot be assumed that those who have been wronged will, upon overturning and gaining power, can, want to, or will do the things that will liberate and improve the conditions of people and places. It cannot be assumed that liberation and improving the conditions of people and places are the reasons for the uprising. The why part, the toward-what-end part, matters.

People arise, people lead, people follow. Who are the people? What are their intentions? Do they come from and sit in the embrace of humanity, even in the fracturing ever-expanding moment of rebellion, or from some other, darker part of human instinct? Coming from this place and conditions in the past, living in this place and conditions in the present, going . . . where, what, and why?

To choose, live by, embrace, and wrest the possibilities of humanity can be a mind-leaping revolutionary act. Choosing humanity and interdependent thriving over other reasons—such as power, wealth, righteousness, control, divinity—may indeed require revolution. But if taken as one set of ideals to merely replace another set of ideals, this revolution is more likely to fail or falter or fail the test of humanity to choose ways of being that are beyond othering.

Scanning the revolution Wikipedia page, we should be worried about the sheer number of righteously well-meaning uprisings. If truly living up to the definition of a giving way to new systems, what is the fault line between our aspirations and sticking the landing to follow through toward wholeness? Perhaps we are unhelpfully caught in the replacement for replacement's sake. Or our so-called revolutionary ideas aren't so. Perhaps we haven't evolved sufficiently to escape a trap of uprising begetting uprising.

The *Oxford* online dictionary provides two definitions for evolution: (1) "the **process** by which different kinds of living organisms are thought to have developed and diversified from earlier forms during the history of the earth"; and (2) "the **gradual development** of something, especially from a simple to a more complex form." *Emphasis added.*

This is the definition. We can even think of evolution as the phenomena that includes and is in between change and transformation.

The theory of evolution includes a key principle that is both scientifically elegant and culturally controversial: the notion of the phenomena of change and transformation most fruitfully occurring in relationship to the change and transformation of the other beings in the natural environment, including the environment itself. This is what Charles Darwin famously observed in the Galápagos Islands. Does it mean evolution was only occurring at that one place in the entire world? No. To become a scientific theory, it couldn't be a one-off, an aberration. The aha! moment became accessible to Darwin because the islands were small ecosystems that contained an abundance of different life forms and species and co-inhabited the ecosystems in relationship with minimal human intervention. The compactness allowed Darwin to efficiently observe and puzzle and narrate. The modern Galápagos experiment is whether interdependent evolution in that place may continue with many more human beings coming and going and staying. The modern Galápagos story is yes, mostly so, if and only if the tortoise gets to do and be what the tortoise needs to do and be rather than the humans' desires overriding and disregarding the being needs of the tortoise. Instead, humans must pay attention to their interactions, as in a dance. For those critical of the snootiness of the tortoise, it is important to note that the humans of the Galápagos do quite well, thank you very much, as tourism and research dollars bloom primarily because the phenomenon of interdependent thriving is still possible to observe and puzzle and delight over.

For the equation lovers who did reasonably well in math and critical problem-solving, think of:

harmonious evolution = (all things interdependently) × (development + diversification)

In harmonious evolution, the beings of a place and time change and transform, adapt and adopt, zig and zag in relationship to each other and the environment in which they live, love, learn. Mostly this happens in an intricate dance over extended periods of time without any engineering . . . except for humans. Humans tend to interfere with the harmony of evolution toward their own needs and ambitions. In the Galápagos, humans endeavor through desire and rule to be as harmonious as they can be. This takes a lot of conscious effort. The traffic will stop for the tortoise making their way across the street. The enterprises of tourism and science provide incentives for the consciousness of stopping for the tortoise. The abundance of natural life is a constant reminder and observable in both struggle and flourishing.

We can both admire and dismiss the Galápagos as special circumstances, an anomaly unlikely to be replicated. We may arrive at this conclusion by virtue of there being very few reproduced models.

Perhaps we're not ambitious enough! Perhaps the Galápagos is the low rung of what's possible. What if the nonhuman world is counting on humans shedding our wanton habits and paying attention to being in an intricate and harmonious dance with each other, as well as other beings, in relationship to the Earth and the Universe? In this kind of evolutionary leap?

The usual slowpoke pace of describable evolution would place an evolutionary leap at the blasphemous side of the scientific scale. In ordinary times, that is. Let's agree we are not in ordinary times. Global environmental phenomena, collapsing economies, mass migration are but a few of the arising and converging meta conditions in which all beings live. There is describable, observable, and measurable evidence of more rapid evolution occurring among nonhuman beings to meet the twin imperative of surviving and thriving. Every month or so, there will be a little article about a plant or animal being thought to have disappeared, only to be found in some part of the earth . . . perhaps many miles away from their usual habitat . . . and doing well, thank you very much, though now sporting different physical and behavioral characteristics than when last seen by humans, and often exhibiting changes during the short duration of observation. Or accelerated migration of lobsters and mangroves, eels and beetles, covering vast territories. All the while, humans will cling stubbornly to the piece of real estate on a crumbling cliff and meet twenty-first-century realities with eighteenth-century frames. Willfully.

There is something about being human, especially a modern human equipped with devices, that makes us less observant of our surroundings, coupled with our absolute belief that we can somehow overcome nature while being saved by (fill in the blank) or not saved and therefore the world as we imagine it will perform as we imagine it. There is a part of who it is we are and how we turned out that is exactly as Yuval Noah Harari described: "Humans are the outcome of blind evolutionary processes that operate without goal or purpose." And there are the consequences when humans meet an extremely consequential Earth moment by operating without goal or purpose.

And so, it would seem, that an accelerated interdependent evolution of who it is we are, how we act, what we believe, what we work to become, will require us to step out of the long blindness and into consciousness.

CHAPTER 10

Eyes Wide Open

In the Rinzai Zen line of my spiritual practice,[4] we sit in meditation with our eyes open.

Huh!?

Sitting dynamically still for forty-five minutes in relaxed concentration, breathing low (in the body) and slow (in pace, and slower on the exhale than on the inhale), with eyes open and relaxed, with a wide field of peripheral vision without moving one's head from side to side or up and down. Yup. Not for the faint of heart or twitchy of butt.

There is no expectation or exhortation for readers to adopt this practice, though I hope you will soon wade into the waters of embodied meditation, or at the least, low and slow breathing. Acknowledging it is a lot to jump into the psychophysical discipline of regular meditation with eyes open, so why do so? Why invite this in a book about what it may take for humanity to evolve, stand, and move into our historic roles of stewardship in this urgent moment?

This timeplace is absolutely an eyes wide open moment. It is a long moment that may indeed span many years. "Eyes wide open" requires objectively paying attention to the quickly evolving phenomena of record-breaking climate events. Vermont has a once-in-a-thousand-year rain in the same week that the Park Fire becomes the fourth largest in California's history. There are head-spinning human events, changing everything in very short periods of time. A president decides in the only window of time left for such a decision to pass the torch. The torch is picked up midair and ignites forty thousand Black women to break Zoom, followed eight days later by hundreds of thousands of white dudes joyfully doing their part. Violence and chicanery move apace in the same news cycle. Sudan crumbles further; Lebanon and Israel exchange bombs and deaths too casually; Maduro claims a win in Venezuela, whether true or not. We pass through anniversaries as time folds upon itself. The sixtieth anniversary of the Civil Rights Act is hailed and mourned for the difference it made and the line's brightness, darkness, near erasure, generational resoluteness. We approach the first anniversary of the tragedy of the fires at Lahaina with solemn gratitude for community, a tear-filled hole of loss, and grim realization of this year's fires sprouting on a too thirsty land. Astronauts remain stranded on the International Space Station, having arrived there on faulty technology. Meanwhile, astrophysicists uncover a massive black hole. And as if all dog lovers don't already know, researchers confirm dogs are impacted by human stress, and in emotional transference will be more hesitant to guard against disappointment. This and much more occupied and passed through the timespace known as the last two weeks in July of the year 2024 on Mother Earth. Eyes wide open.

We are the humans living in the swiftly moving current much of which has been exacerbated by humans and human actions over time and space. This phenomenon is shorthandedly called *collective acceleration*. We cannot afford to keep our eyes closed. This is not a thrill ride in which we, the humans, can afford to close our eyes, knuckle grip the seat bar, and scream as our stomachs rise, or drop, as the case may be.

Wehewehe.org, the online Hawaiian dictionary, defines maka'ala, as "alert, vigilant, watchful, wide awake; to attend to vigilantly." This describes what it is I mean by eyes wide open. To do otherwise would be for us to be the humans who are sleeping on the job in a consequential, generational moment. Instead, e makaʻala mai i ka hana! Tend to the job! The tending to the job part of makaʻala is the action part of having one's eyes wide open. No use alertly observing, only to be a bystander. Shameful for ancestors of descendants yet to come.

With eyes wide open, we can tend to the job at hand. To be clear, having eyes wide open includes more than one's sight. Are we listening, not only hearing? What are we listening to and from whom? Are we quiet enough inside of us to not rush to the sound of our judgment and, instead, hear and listen to the subtext, that which is not said, the barely articulate yet poetically true? What are we feeling? Not only in the region of our own emotions, but also in our guts, our naʻau, the core of our intuitive knowing? Is this way cool, or too hot to touch? Does something smell fishy, or rotten, or bitter, or sweet, or bittersweet? If so, probably so. Is it so close we can taste it? Then it is indeed close, and we should not hesitate for even a nano moment. If neither seeing, hearing, feeling, smelling, or tasting, then how can we say we are perceiving what is in front of us right now, let alone down the twisty road? Makaʻala!

With eyes wide open, we can tend to the job at hand. We can see, feel, and begin to understand what in front of us is unfolding. Sometimes s-l-o-w-l-y, nearly imperceptibly, and sometimes so quickly that if we momentarily close our eyes, everything will have changed. The important aspect is to perceive that which is in front of us is continuing to change. That is an unwavering law of the universe. Last night, there was a very real possibility of rolling shutdowns of the electrical grid across Honolulu. At 2 p.m. the utility announced the possibility based on an unexpected shutdown of an independent power plant that supplies power to the utility. Based on supply and demand estimates, there would not be enough supply for the usual demand, beginning at 5 p.m. and through the evening till about 9 p.m. A news alert went out to folx warning of the probability of controlled blackouts from thirty minutes to an hour, naming area by area, and asking folx to conserve electricity to lessen the probability. It was announced the areas would include large commercial users and individual users, residences, and hotels. The area recently hit by multiple days of electrical outage due to other issues would not be included in the rolling shutdown plan. Less than an hour later, an additional release was sent out by the water utility. It takes a lot of electricity to pump water, so folx were asked to conserve water, to use water for cooking, drinking, and personal hygiene, but please hold off washing clothes, watering plants, washing your car, power-washing your driveway, changing the water in the koi pond, backyard water-sliding in the late afternoon. In my small household, my sister returned from work early to drizzle a little water on the flowers and bathe California-style, involving a quick wet-down, turning off the water while lathering up, and turning on the water, vigorously washing off whether or not the water has had time to heat up. Earlier I had checked the batteries in the LED lamps and filled a few pots with water for drinking and toilet flushing. Oh, we also cooked rice because in our household, having cooked rice is the indicator of our readiness for whatever may come. We ate early—a meal requiring not much electricity, just a quick bok choy stir fry, and ahi poke mixed with an abundance of seaweed, with our rice, and fresh fruit, keeping the refrigerator and freezer tightly closed. I too took a California-style shower, powered up my sister's smart-kine phone and my flip-kine phone, unplugged our laptops from the possibility of power surges, and went to bed early.

As it turns out, the utility was able to bring back online a unit that was down for scheduled maintenance to make up for some of the projected supply deficit. It will be another two to three days before the independent power plant is back online, so our conservation and emergency measures need to continue without taking last night's near-miss as the guaranteed outcome. It will be interesting to see what the actual water and electricity consumptions were in the eighteen hours after the public announcements. Did we, small and large households, tourists and restaurants, graduation parties and shopping malls, did we take what measures we could to conserve and put in place the measures to usefully weather rolling blackouts if they came to be? Were all of our combined efforts just enough or more than enough to make it unnecessary for the utility to ration power? Makaʻala. See what is in front of us as it unfolds, and do what is necessary, as it unfolds.

I woke up to the absence of blinking reset lights on the various devices and internet box, and the news of the release of long-held prisoners, including Evan Gershkovich, Paul Whelan, Alsu Kurmasheva, Vladimir Kara-Murza, and Russian citizens imprisoned for their dissent. I watched a national security advisor make the announcement from the White House press briefing podium and inadvertently lose his composure, requiring a brief pause while a gentle moist wave of relief and gladness and gratitude passed over and through him. How long must this human and innumerable folx, including the families, friends, and colleagues of Evan Gershkovich, Paul Whelan, Alsu Kurmasheva, and Vladimir Kara-Murza, have had to keep their eyes wide open? Details are still arriving. What we know so far is complex, involving the release of twenty-four individuals, seven countries, multiple personal conversations between heads of state, difficult conversations internal to countries as they weighed the risks and values in the release of this person and not including this person, steadily, frustratingly, tediously, persistently over years. Just when they thought they were close, Alexei Navalny tragically died under opaque circumstances, dashing hopes of his freedom being a part of the complex equation. Back to scratch, reshuffle the deck, rebuilding with what they could, and landing on tarmacs domestic and foreign. This intricate diplomacy required a level of disciplined and discerning maka'ala by professionals, in relationship to political leaders, each dealing with their own domestic and foreign problems. We have become sadly accustomed to the exchange of prisoners. We may not appreciate the thinking and work to see possibilities beyond a tit for tat. Secretary of State Antony Blinken described the feat this way: "Sometimes enlarging the problem is the key to success." To see beyond what is directly in front of you, while knowing what is right in front of you.

There is the seeing, and there is the making happen. Patient, persistent, problem-solving initiative while holding the whole is part of the inner workings of tending to the job of eyes wide open. In the story still unfolding of this one knot loosening is the matter-of-fact acknowledgment of the importance of relationship. The public statements, given the season, are crafted around alliances and ties between countries and leaders of countries. What it boils down to are people talking (and talking and talking) with one another to make it happen. Never giving up. And some of those people knew each other, trusted each other, respected each other, and knew with eyes wide open that not all the players would be able to be trusted and had done nothing to earn respect. For those who did, those with pilina, with interwoven relationship, they mutually aimed toward holding the whole when others may not, and made it happen. This time. Building a bit of ground and hope for the next time. And so a longtime professional would stand at a podium and tears would arise. **May we never forget why and for whom.** This, too, being maka'ala, eyes wide open.

CHAPTER 11

Discipline, Discipline, Discipline

Good morning! Did you remember to say good morning to the beings, including close humans, including co-workers, today? To the people whose names you do not know though you see them every day driving the bus, delivering the mail, making your coffee? Did you mean it? Good morning. It is a simple thing. The discipline of this is a practice, really, of greeting the day as much as the beings, including close humans, including co-workers.

Did you fix your bed? I am not good at that piece, having left it behind many years ago. Even I need to adjust the pillow, tend to my pjs, make sure my sheets are clean, especially in the summer when the weather tends to get a bit sticky, even back in Kalihi Valley. This place, this bed, after all, is a place of rest. It should be ready for my next time of rest when I return to it. A bed greets you but has no agency to fix itself up. Most of us don't have servants. Serving the bed serves us.

What is the very first thing you do? After turning off the alarm or ooshing the pet out of the tangled way or awakening one's partner, or grumbling about being awakened, what is the next thing? For most of us, it isn't fixing your bed. It is some form of personal hygiene, including but not limited to a close encounter with plumbing. A good thing! A very good thing for all of the beings we will subsequently be in relationship to, and a good thing to notice the small things about our face and teeth and eyes and bodies we don't necessarily pay attention to, let alone attend to, for the remainder of our waking hours. Therefore, put down that device! No device, no phone, no iPad, no iWatch or whatever they call the Dick Tracy device, no social media of any kind, no news feed before tending to one's personal hygiene. How can you maka'ala with maka piapia,[5] the crusted secretions, in your eyes?

The time of one's arising is one of the most precious times in daily existence. Assuming you have rested reasonably well—a note about the discipline of resting can be found near the end of this chapter—the mind and body have been given the makana, the gift, of a reset. That doesn't mean it is reset like the device recharging all night. There is a thing called stretching. Most beings stretch naturally after being still for any length of time, let alone all night long. Most beings, even protozoa, stretch naturally, luxuriously, except for humans, who mysteriously stop after the age of six or so. We need a reminder or a practice of stretching. Even if we get up a bit stiff and creaky, which, by the way for those of you who are under the age of thirty, will happen regularly soon enough. The mind and the body and the spirit are hardwired together, with an emphasis on hardwire versus Bluetooth, and mind and spirit have far less connectivity and elasticity when our body is stiff and creaky. It is true at some point in one's life stiff and creaky will be the norm. So to be less stiff and less creaky, please stretch.

The time of one's arising is one of the most precious times in daily existence. After personal hygiene, after stretching, after resetting one's nest, after a drink of water to break the fast, the quiet of one's spirit will greet you. Good morning. It is the most precious reflective moment. Reflection is a thing that happens when you can see the light of the moon shimmering on the quiet surface of a pond. Reflection isn't talking talking talking about the light of the moon shimmering on the quiet surface of a pond. Being the quiet surface—and depth—of a pond for just a bit will expand you and ground you. Don't worry, you'll remember everything that has flooded or seductively tiptoed into your cognitive mind now that you are rested. No need to rush there. You will be only there soon enough. For this moment, the precious time of one's arising, spend more than a few moments in the slowness and lowness of your breath. Even for those who do not have regular meditation practice, just stretch slowly, taking your breath along the fullness of each move, exhaling longer than the inhale and lower in your body. How low? Surely nothing above your belly should be rising and falling, and having the whole region of your gut and bellybutton and stomach just be a slow-motion bellows would be a good thing. In and o-u-t. In and o-u-t. For those who have meditation practice, whatever it may be, this is the very best time to be breathing in your still body connected to the moment-by-moment arising of the day's light. Even if your regular meditation time is at another time of the day, even a few minutes of breathing in your still body newly stretched will just reconnect everything in your body you have taken for granted.

There is something about the morning that calls for a beverage. I am not a smoothie kind of person, but I do acknowledge that it is a morning beverage thing. The coffees, the chai, the teas, cocoa, milk, and juice. We savor this morning beverage. What!? Don't you savor the morning beverage?! Savor! Without regret. With luck, those first few sips will extend the morning silence. In any case, the first sips are the first conscious hydration of the day. If we take it consciously, the practice helps us to hydrate consciously throughout the day. Not remembering to regularly hydrate is a common human error in which hour by hour we suboptimize our performance and put our one body at risk. Conscious hydration is particularly important as the earth warms. Conscious hydration includes having an understanding and making good decisions about what we drink. There is no substitute for water. (Please care for and protect your water!) Sugary drinks don't have less sugar just because you're pouring it in rather than chewing on it or are paying eighty times more per unit than gasoline. Be safe and moderate about your alcohol consumption as consciousness counts. Caffeinated drinks don't hydrate as well as water. There is no substitute for water. (Please care for and protect your water!)

How do you break your fast? As it turns out, the morning beverage goes a long way toward useful and responsible lubrication prior to introducing solid foods. The savored morning beverage breaks the fast. To break the fast, there needs to be a fast. Not eating too late into the night, having a short sleep—a long nap, really, getting up early and gobbling the reheated breakfast burrito. The duration of the daily fast matters and will be different for different bodies. Do you know what your body needs? Not only by reading up the AI chatbot. Consciously experiment with the indicators of energy and gut ease. Most bodies, which by hardwired definition include body-mind-spirit, are regulated by the stomach. My day will vary in its rhythm and intensity if I do the breakfast-lunch-dinner thing or whether I do the brunch–light snack–light dinner thing. Having the discipline to sit and just eat is critical. Mindful chewing does not require slow chewing unless the mechanics of one's jaw and tongue and swallowing apparatus require it to be so. Just sitting and eating is a gift to your body and mind, more enjoyable in even the simplest of fare, easier on the gut. And for those who reflexively eat at your desk, remember two things. First, mindlessly gobbling while continuing to work encourages a higher caloric intake because you're more likely drawn to the easiest and therefore not the most nutritious thing. Second, research has shown the average work desk has at least the same amount of if not more germy stuff as the average public toilet seat. Just saying. Reflexiveness does not equate to discipline.

By the way, what do you eat? What you eat matters as much as when you eat. Most folx who live in America consume too much sugar and too much salt. An increase in sugar consumption per capita is one of the signs of growth in prosperity of the nation. Perversely, at a certain level of national prosperity, the cheaper fast foods will have among the highest levels of sugar + salt. Eat more whole foods (by definition, not by brand) and fewer processed foods. What you eat matters. If the food available to you is because it is cheaper, closer, you lack refrigeration or a stove, are by yourself momentarily in many moments, less than able, then awareness, access, and alternatives are paramount. What we eat matters individually and societally.

Enjoyment is a complex satiation, so interrupt the habit of bluntly rewarding with sugar + salt + fat or the-more-the-better. As a cook, I practice bringing out the various dimensions of taste and textures, for even a clear soup with simple ingredients will have complexity in depth. Do you cook? What?! You don't cook?! Not even one meal a week?! Okay. Interrupting judgment here, my overuse of question marks and exclamation points is much more an expression of concern. The simple preparation of one's own food on a regular basis is a complex embodied practice that is almost always less expensive, fresher, more satisfying. Put down the device. Take the time. Everyone over the age of twelve should know how to make a simple meal for themselves and for others.

Have you embraced casual dress every-day-of-the-week? Hard not to as an island resident, or a mostly work-from-homer. Even in the environment and circumstances of branded casual, there is presentation. As a mostly work-from-homer, this means virtual meetings. The people I meet with deserve the professionalism as if a meeting were to be in person. (At least from the waist up, that is. There are useful accommodations in practice, after all.) For me, this may mean changing multiple times in a day for different meetings, or to take out messy trash, or to be comfortable without air conditioning, or comfortable if the weather cools 10 degrees. This is a discipline of paying attention inside-outside-inside. As a useful by-product, there isn't as much angst or inappropriateness when I am traveling (… hint: both waist up and waist down need to be appropriate, including with each other) or going downtown. Works well with no maka piapia. Don't assume Norma is a prim and proper dresser. My mail carrier knows the truth. The mailbox is the farthest boundary of who-cares-what-I'm-wearing-as-long-as-I'm-wearing. Nevertheless, my teeth and short hair will be brushed, no maka piapia, no pjs to the mailbox. Hey. I respect my mail carriers, who not only deliver my mail and pick up my packages. They say, "Good morning!," "Good afternoon!," smile, and nod in recognition. Disrespectful to gross them out.

Working all hours of the day and days of the week is a thing. In my case, this is driven by time differences—six hours behind the US East Coast, twelve hours from France, two hours ahead of New Zealand, plus work ethic. Luckily, I am not on the hyperdrive and interstitial syncopation of social media. While I do text, it is a laborious thing with my preferred flip phone device and, therefore, discourages reflexive around-the-clock texts. Still, time differences and work ethic extend work hours, requiring discipline to ensure my energy and mind remain sharp and don't become lulled into the false stimulus of doingness. Adherence to the 20-20-20 rule, for example. No staring at any screen for more than twenty minutes without looking at least twenty feet away for at least twenty seconds. Sitting no more than ninety minutes. Getting up and stretching at least every ninety minutes, or refilling my water, or visiting the fruit bowl, or checking the laundry, or washing my cup, or picking up the thing in the corner, or stretching. Reducing the sit time in the afternoon. Taking longer moments to prepare a meal, sweep the leaves out of the garage, lie down for twenty minutes, wash my hair in the sink. Don't try to write or respond creatively when the brain is tired and thoughts swirl in fuzzy sluggishness. Sip hydrate. Cut off the beloved tea early enough in the afternoon to ensure a better night's rest. When I am sitting and working, to just work. No forays into the news feed, Minesweeper, *New Yorker* cartoons, or sister-sent-to-flip-phone-memes. Focus! Less process and more focus. Short, clear responses. Don't say more when less will do. Say more when less will not. Thoughtful responses when thoughtful responses are called for by thoughtful inquiries. It is true that if I were in a consulting firm there would be an abundance of billable hours. Work ethic, after all. But not while I am eating—at home or in a restaurant. Not while I am meeting with someone else, for business or for friendship or for pleasure. Not when I am making or drinking a proper pot of tea, or one of my sister's artisanal mocktails. Not if I am shopping for groceries or socks.[6] Not if I am engaged in practice or meditation. Not while I am driving, or parking, or waiting at a stop light. One thing at a time. Work deserves its due.

A life of discipline does not mean one doesn't have a portfolio of habits. Habits—unconscious repetitive actions—will be with us always, like cockroaches. Habits neutrally obscure. Since the body and mind act unconsciously, a so-called good habit never optimizes its usefulness. If you put your keys in that one place regularly and rather mindlessly, you'll lose it the moment you place your keys somewhere else. Brushing your teeth twice a day is great for the specific teeth that do get properly brushed, and not so great for the teeth and gums that are habitually missed, twice a day. So-called bad habits wear a rut into our psyche, are perversely comforting, part of our identity and defensive armor. We are who we are. This is a truism, not only a Zenism. And yet, the conscious part of who we are always has choice. It is always possible to lean into a more fruitful and less defensive path. It is more probable with conscious interruption, one persnickety habit at a time! Habits almost always have a physical manifestation. Those are the ones we can see both during and after the act. The footwear haphazardly underfoot. The (fill in the blank) left (fill in the blank) or discarded before its time or clung to beyond its usefulness. The twitch or tightening of the (fill in the blank) muscle whenever (name the person) inevitably says what (name the person) says. The twitch or tightening will be accompanied by a thought habitually arising in our mind, in reflexive response to what (name the person) has said for the zillionth time. Even now we can recall the provocation, our thoughts, and the body's reaction. Or we can be that person. Not you, of course. Speaking for myself. I can be that person who is always saying "x" or "y" or "z," both igniting and responding to an endless chain of habits. Habits live in the stew of unconsciousness, reinforcing our isolation from what is right in front of us and increasing the difficulty of seeing around the bend. Interrupting habits frees us, opens us, sheds baggage. Habits don't like being set aside, requiring daily, lighthearted vigilance. The interruption of habits is the discipline's useful grist.

While habits are unconscious repetitive acts, practices are conscious repetitive acts. Practice is what makes a natural talent great and finds awesomeness without talent. Without practice, a natural talent will be without dimension, may become indulgent, and in retrospect feel wasted. Without practice, art and craft and skill never hone. Without consciousness, repetitive acts are clones, derivatives, mechanical. Consciousness adds discernment, desire, interrupts useless acts and behaviors. Consciousness in practice reveals our beingness, our truer selves, one practice at a time. Practice is both hard and joyous, and simply unable to be done without internal discipline. Fruitful practice is one of the ways you practice discipline. We are familiar with the role of practice in sports, music, art, baking, cooking, dancing, martial arts, writing . . . As it turns out, nearly everything in one's life can be practiced and honed. Nearly everything we practice is transferable to other aspects of our lives. Therefore, practice in ways that are generative, with discipline but not obsessively, critically but without eye-narrowing judgment. Be in practice for the long haul. I have cooked since my teens and practiced cooking since my mid-twenties. Meditation in the form known as zazen began in earnest just before my thirtieth birthday. My kado—way of the flower—practice is now twenty-four years in, and shodo—way of the brush—practice a young twenty years, the same vintage as the 10-Step Tai Chi form developed by Dogi Kow Roshi. Chanting is arguably older than twenty-four years, depending on how I define chanting. Cooking will always have primacy because the actions of this practice feed me and my small household each day. My most consistent daily practice occurred during the pandemic, a record 475 consecutive days of preparing at least two meals a day for my small household, usefully resetting our gut but also developing nuanced understanding of complexity without difficulty or complication. The overlay of cooking, zazen and breath, kado, shodo, 10-Step Tai Chi, and chanting inform each other while strengthening characteristics of reflective quiet, focus, interrupting hesitation and doubt, plumbing depth, centeredness without dogma, perspective, discipline. Except for breath, I do not do all these practices every day. There is regularity, not dailiness. My practices gathered over time, and some—like shodo—were surprises. One need not have as many. Breath is fundamental. Please practice breath. And in an embodied practice way, having both physical practice and art practice triangulates our awareness.

The crossover between practice and discipline is simple. Practice without discipline is not practice at all. And with discipline, anything you do is practice.

Like resting, for example. Our bodies and our minds need regular rest. If we tend to rest in each twenty-four-hour cycle, just as Earth does, then we are moving in the rhythm of the universe and tending to the remarkable regenerative qualities of the human body and spirit. If we habitually operate in a deficit, the wear and tear on our bodies and minds and spirits multiplies. We can also become accustomed to this state of aches, fatigue, forgetfulness, ever-present toxicity, and drift further away from the revelatory ahas available on the windward side of rest. Tending to rest in each twenty-four-hour cycle requires discipline. There is always something else to do, somewhere else to be. Always. Interrupting rest becoming a victim to urgency takes discipline. A leader I worked for was a master at taking refreshing fifteen-minute catnaps on the way to an event. Most of us don't have personal drivers on demand. Therefore, a restful night is even more important. Dehydration can tire us out. Regular hydration also serves as a function in whether our bodies and minds receive the full benefit of a restful night. Rest is impeded by habits we may have in the golden hour prior to sleeping. This should be a ramp down on everything period of time, rather than a rush to finish and cram all of the electronics time. For those of a certain age at both ends of the human life, naps are not only good, they're also great! For most adults, shorter naps rest the body and mind without interrupting the circadian rhythm. Some folx shower prior to sleeping. Some folx awaken in the shower. Water upon us is not only good hygiene. There is soothing connectivity in water ablutions. For the day-shower folx, at least wash one's face, neck, arms, (various pits), and the bottom of your feet. You'll feel better, and rest better.

From arising to resting. This chapter could have gone on and on in the many ways our daily activity is littered with unconsciousness on the one hand, and a multitude of opportunities for practice in which the discipline of practice serves us. But what's the point of discipline in the human construct?

Without discipline and the discipline of practice, it is nearly impossible for consciousness to be one's primary state of being, let alone our collective state of being. Left to our own devices, literally, we will drift, meandering from one dazzling distraction to another grievance. Focus and intention and purpose are learned, capable of honing and accelerating. Our discipline and willingness to lean into whatever it is we need to interrupt and whatever it is we need to create, with eagerness, is the hard work we need. If we are to evolve.

CHAPTER 12

Cultivation of the Human Spirit

In his debut as a national figure, Governor and vice presidential nominee Tim Walz turned to his running mate and exclaimed, "Thank you for bringing back the joy!" And the overflowing crowd cheered, shouted, clapped, jumped up and down, and raised their faces to the sky. Several political reporters, not known for their spontaneity, were caught unawares by the lightness of their own voices in reporting this news. It was as if a great weight had been lifted, even from those who were professionally trained in matter-of-factness.

Being human means we are normally impacted by what is going on around us, in us, among us. We profoundly experience dread, dragging us, dampening us, and we profoundly experience happiness, expanding us, affirming us. This isn't only a description of our emotional state. There is an ephemeral yet very real and essential elemental state of humanness, the living energy and well-being of our individual and collective spirit.

In defining "spirit," I am drawn and influenced by these three aspects described in the *Merriam-Webster* online dictionary: ". . . an animating or vital principle held to give life to physical organisms . . .

the immaterial intelligent or sentient part of a person . . . [and] the activating or essential principle influencing a person." We, of course, can feel what spirit is just as we may have our own personal understanding of it. This inquiry focuses on this specific combination of spirit's attributes—the animation, vital principle, and sentience of spirit essential to life itself—and the how and why our cultivation of these attributes is foundational to the present and future of humanity.

One of the wondrous aspects of spirit is its impact on our excitement and energy. When our spirits are "up," we are buoyed. When our spirits are "down," we are heavy. It cannot be definitively said whether excitement and energy are present because of the state of our spirits, or the other way around. Who cares when we are so happy! Does it matter if we are sad? It nevertheless can be measured. Think of the changes in the volume of noise during a game as the fortune of teams ebbs and flows. And the profound nothingness when teams dud out. There is a felt sense of an increase in the mass of bodies, hardly contained, excitement propelling arms into the air, bodies out of seats, hearts pumping. It is difficult to not be excited in such an environment. Attending as an uninformed plus one, you'll be caught up in it all and find yourself yelling whatever may be the chant of the moment. There is an acceleration of more-ness. A moment later, you may ask: What just happened?! Why are we yelling? The very sound of happy shouting attracts an energetic pull, just as music—soft or loud, instrumental or voice—encircles us by filling the room, the space, with tangible vibration.

Our rational mind comes along for the ride of our spirit, which is not rational at all. The theoretical outcome of an event, as measured by whatever measurements you may find and believe, is the same if your spirits are high or if they are low. But what a difference possibility makes. A felt sense of possibility—not a rational notion of possibility—generates action in the direction of the possibility. A human with a pattern of quiet emotions may not be as demonstrative in their spirited exclamations, but nonetheless feel compelled to act in furtherance of possibility. Your spirit oxygenates your muscles, creating a tunnel in which it is possible to traverse mostly unimpeded through your doubt or fear or suspicion.

The part of us that perceives and feels, the part that is sentient, is both spirit generator and spirit itself. Our spirit perceives and feels. It is both right thumb over left thumb *and* left thumb over right thumb. It occupies the timespace of both at the same moment, not one and then the other, which is a logic-defying feat. When every single sense we have, including but not limited to our common senses, are firing on all cylinders at the same time, an energy fills every part of our being, all the organs, our mindspace empties and expands, and **We. Know.**

We know what?! At that moment, it doesn't matter and it entirely matters. The "it" isn't brought through some long process of our thinking. It Just Is.

It is light. And warm. The light has no weight but is voluminous nonetheless, glowing just rightly, occasionally very brightly. The warmth knows to keep in just the right realm of embracing comfort, occasionally spiking (but to be clear that's mostly about all of the other folx around us who are also generating heat and, clearly, we overdressed).

Spirit is clarifying. It shows us the path forward . . . if we are listening. How spirit accomplishes this feat only matters for those who are overusing their right thumb over left thumb, which by the way can happen to the left thumb over right thumbers as well.

Humans being human, messing up the spirit thing is a thing. We can easily forget there are other aspects making up who it is we are, that become untethered or exclusive. Just because there is light-ness in spirit doesn't mean it is ever useful for us to float away like a helium-filled balloon. Balls of our feet on the ground, wriggling toes knowing the contours of Mother Earth, life-giving breath low in our bodies and slow on the exhale, head up so we may see the horizon and therefore where it is we are going and why . . . This is the useful and well-maintained vessel for spirit-led existence.

Spirit is a powerful life force and is best held with love, respect, and mature choices. The responsibility of adults is to cherish and cultivate the spirit of young'uns, irrespective of our biological relat-edness. A raison d'être of young'uns is to activate the part of adult spirit that is the child within them, the part that feels the knowing of no bounds and suddenly understands that practicality and possi-bility are not a binary. This mutuality is essential to the well-being of individuals, a lifeblood of communities, and a treasure of nation-states. The strength and reciprocity of the bond is a litmus test of the health of humanity.

Connection and care are natural aspects of spirit, a great cur-rent that feeds and nourishes the giver and the given. When we are in relationship with other beings, perceive what is useful and needed, and act in furtherance of their well-being, our spirits are both leading and receiving. To both give and to receive with grace and wisdom is a conscious act. Conscious acts are furthered with practice. Taking that moment and not brushing it away usefully resets our rhythm and, therefore, our capacity to perceive and understand. Gratitude flows, for ourselves and for other beings, internally and externally not as a binary but as a regenerative flow.

Spirit can fill us in entirety even when we are grieving. The ea, the spirit air, liquefies and combines with all the waters within us, gathering again and again as a great tidal flow, spilling over as a reservoir will when rain has fallen for many days. Within us, the tears that are becoming wash through every corner of our being, cleansing, caressing. Even if there are no other beings near us at that moment, we will feel closeness and missing at the same time. The world as we know it becomes very still as breath and water mingle. There is a fullness in this spirit.

We can and should cultivate spirit. We can and must guard against quashing, denying, taking for granted the spirit that is our most precious life force. When our spirit energy is low, the light of our eyes dulled, purpose leaves the house. Without purpose, we begin to wander or circle, repeat and forget, not notice the many things that begin to accumulate. We become the humans on flat tires, struggling to make our way. Paradoxically, low spirit energy requires more energy to do everything.

Sometimes I am blue, neither light nor dark. It is impossible to know whether it is tiredness of the mind, the body, or the spirit. Indeed, it does not matter as we are literally hardwired. Low spirits can recover, renewed in rest, brightened in color, beckoned with deliciousness, refill as the sun returns. Except for a few exceptional beings, it is simply not possible to always be in "great" spirits. Sometimes we are, and sometimes we are not. If we are to be mostly so, let it be in the hopeful range.

Without hope, we become prey to baser instincts. Our feelings and logic lose their mooring. When low spirits dip into the red line of our spiritual meter and approach nadir, the air leaves us. "Deflated," we sigh. Darkness hovers, even at midday. At a certain point, we will grasp and chase anything. Our energy shifts from the prefrontal cortex to the amygdala and we are drawn to the magnetic pull of energetic external influences.

The absence of spirit is the field in which violence grows. No air. No light. Both devoid of warmth and engulfed in searing heat. This is the burrowing of humanity just before its implosive end.

The present and future of humanity depends on the flourishing of our collective spirit. Within us, yes. Between us, yes. Between and among, in and out, ever expanding, a warm and cooling current. We tend not to prioritize cultivation in urgent times. And yet, what would we eat if the farmers among us stopped?

As individuals, there is much to do and be in furtherance of spirit hygiene. Our minds and bodies and spirits are hardwired. When we are dementedly overprocessing, our spirit has no place to enter. When our bodies are chronically stressed, dehydrated, forgotten as mere vessels of our desires, our spirits are unconsciously working in overdrive to compensate for our suffering bodies. The principle of interdependent wholeness begins with us, literally. In furtherance of spirit health, there are things to do, and things to not do, things to practice, and things to interrupt. Spaciousness is the timeplace of spirit possibilities. Cultivation of spaciousness requires consciousness and, frequently, the discipline of choosing what we take on, what we set aside, what we delegate, what we wait for rather than chase. Spirit-embraced spaciousness begins with a well-placed pause, a life-giving sip, an unctuous bite, and, most importantly, a conscious series of breaths.

Contact with beings connects our spirit to more than our own individual existence. Yes, connect with other humans . . . even if to just observe them from afar (in physical reality, not in media). And remember the uncomplicated contacts possible with other-than-human beings. The Japanese have popularized *shinrin-yoku,* forest bathing; sojourns through the forest in which one just experientially connects with all of one's senses, to "wash" oneself, renew one's spirit. Walking along a stream, we hear and see the movement we need to break through spirit stuckness. Even lifting one's head from the labor of the moment to rest one's eyes in the sight of flowers, the desert's deceptive emptiness, the tree outside the window that needs trimming, an inquisitive squirrel will tease us from isolation. No butterfly will make it to the next nectar-filled cup while carrying a backpack of rocks. Our urgent list has no end. Just drop the rocks, one by one, and the bag itself, if one can. The work is easier, faster, without the self-imposed burden.

We are indeed more than our own individual existence, and, in fact, it is impossible for any of us to long survive by ourselves, each isolated doing all of the things for ourselves and only for ourselves. Yes, there are such folx. But it is literally impossible for the eight-plus billion people on Earth to live, let alone prosper, totally by ourselves, one by one by one. Our spirits lift when we are doing the hard work together, side by side, each in accordance with their own ability and yet stretching beyond into that in-between space that makes us all much more than our individual parts, our individual contributions. The Sufi say, in the equation of $1 + 1$, do not underestimate the $+$.

Indeed, these times of accelerated collapse beckon from, call out to, gather our collective spirit. There is a mysterious wonder when we are One with each other. Simply unexplainable. Even I, a documented introvert, will be inwardly joyous though I prefer to celebrate next door to the main party, to dimly hear the noise, to be unencumbered from the necessity of conversation. In this slightly distant state, I too am a part of the collective spirit.

Relearning how to be with each other, to be with other beings, is key to our collective cultivation. It is simple, but not easy. Too many things have been learned and baked into our behavioral and thought patterns. We simply do not take the time to pause, and just connect. Our lack of practice makes it awkward, weird even, to acknowledge someone we do not know for no other reason than to just connect. This is not networking, or courtesy, or manners, or building relationships, or organizing. It is much more basic than any of these things. It is primal contact. The acknowledgment of a living being to another living being, human or not, friend or not, foe or not. It begins with the briefest gazes in which energy passes in the intervening space. The contact may be made without notice. Or it may be a simultaneous acknowledgment. A sharing of breath. We see each other, and it is enough, for now.

CHAPTER 13

Forget Presence, Be Conscious

Being present is a great thing. In the tournament of life, one must be present to win. And it isn't enough! Not in a timespace on the precipice of devolution. We are called to be conscious.

What does it mean to be conscious? I am drawn to the definition in the *Collins* online dictionary, which "implies to be awake or awakened to an inner realization of a fact, a truth, a condition." Beyond seeing, observing, sensing, consciousness allows us to be awakened to that part of us that **knows**. When we makaʻala, see what is in front of us as it unfolds and are called to do what is necessary, as it unfolds, we must be more than present, we must be fully in our conscious selves.

Some people hear the word "conscious" and think or instinctively feel "conscience"; you know, that thing in you that says what is "right" and what is "wrong." That is way too much thought! In fact, to be conscious is to interrupt thought. Here we are going for the whole of you that is well-honed by your collective experience and learnings through timespace, and in relationship to other beings, family, friends, colleagues, intimates, and foes. Everyone has consciousness, which encompasses the unearthing, the emergence, the shining the light on that which we just accumulate or filter through unconsciously. There is no hard barrier between conscious and unconscious. Think and experience consciousness and unconsciousness as a spectrum, an ombré. On one end, one is awake, and the other not. A part available, another not so much. Active, and inert. Alive, and dormant. Energy glowing here, quietly simmering there. There is directional possibility in consciousness, a naturally static nature in the unconscious. While consciousness has conscience, what good is conscience if otherwise dormant, static, inert? In fact, conscience is but one of several internal steering devices that constitute a gyroscope[7] of sorts, that we may be free to alter actions and directions as circumstances require while remaining stable and true at our center. Discerning compassion. Earned wisdom. Mutual responsibility. Embodied conscience.

In service of consciousness, we must acknowledge the ways modernity conspires to obscure this core component of sentience, all the while conflating adrenaline-fueled alertness with being conscious. True awakeness requires unconfused activation. In many ways, our spongelike capacity to addictively absorb all the information of the day crowds out our consciousness. Being "full of it" is not a compliment. We have blinders from listening only to those voices we agree with. Or confusion from facts canceling facts, beliefs trumping beliefs. Or numbness from the firehose of dueling noise. Or selective memory as a coping mechanism in the riptide of fast-moving events.

The constancy of noise obscures the data points of "what is" and defends itself against efforting into "what can be." The relative quiet and vastness of space is required for consciousness to interrupt the habits and dependence on noise. Quiet is relative because when one is truly conscious there is no such thing as no sound in any natural space-place. A walk on a deserted trail, all senses tingling, crunch of our feet on the uneven path, insects buzz and click, a very slight breeze brushes grasses against each other, something larger moved suddenly, there, to the left, and suddenly you are aware that your breath has increased in volume, somehow. Even in a hermetically sealed room there will likely be a mechanical hum from the lights. Avoid the hermetically sealed room. A relatively quiet urban scape with children's sports-playing in the distance, leash jangling dogs leading owners, the occasional harrumphing pickup, idling gas eater, whirling EV can be as useful a backdrop to tease out consciousness, if you turn off the electronics, put down the endless commentaries, and still the twitch.

The present is the most fleeting of all times. To be conscious, we face forward, while knowing that which preceded us. Being present can be a long, delicious moment if uncluttered, unfettered. And just like that, by definition, the present moment has passed. Presence is the temporary timespace-bound moment that sits within a nearly unlimited expanse of consciousness. Consciousness is bigger, elastic, encompassing that which has been, that which is, and that which will be. It is dynamic. We move in the direction of the current we feel-see-hear-know, embracing both awesome strength and awesome kuleana, the mutual responsibility we hold because we have the agency of consciousness.

Those who fear the collapse of humanity can go off the rails. Alternatively, we can recognize that here and now, in the event horizon where we feel and know humanity is in danger, here is the critical juncture when and where change begins. There can be no stronger impetus for the cultivation of inner knowing as the disciplined practice we deserve. And our inner life will make a difference if it emanates outward. Nothing conscious about a stone Buddha, my teacher would say. Don't just sit there!

CHAPTER 14

A Reflection

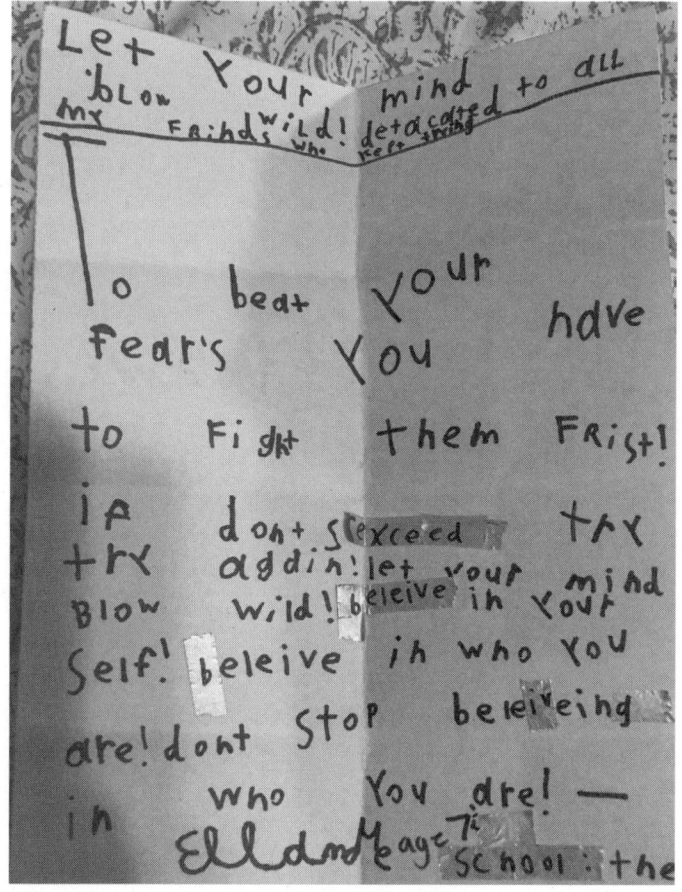

Some thing stirs
In this one possibility
Will we arise to recognize
Who we are
Matters
Yes, we said
Who we are
Though tightly bound
In our otherness phase
Really what matters
Is whether we will see a human
When we look in the mirror
At the human looking in the mirror
Holding the mirror
Behind our shoulder
Yet another
And another
Human
Innumerable
Reflections
Of humans
And do we know what that means?
At this threshold
Where fundamental change may still be possible
Before we cross the threshold
Of the horizon of loss
So profound
It cannot be recovered
The event horizon
Of collapse

Revealing
As only collapse can
Walls dividing
Unable to meet
Piko a piko
Bellybutton to bellybutton
Alo a he alo
Face to face
Not the same
As in your face
No meeting here
In tolerance barely sufficient
Acceptance opens a tightly guarded door
Relationship tackles problems
Mutuality bears fruit
Interdependence reveals
The jeweled core of who we are
Beings
Wondering
Who we are
Wandering
Without purpose
So attenuated from
Our original beingness
A jeweled core
Humming
With bright light
Fierce in joy
Prayerful courage
Discerning

Judgment not judged
Just seen
That which cannot be seen[8]
Hearing what cannot be heard
Knowing the unknowable
This way of being
A jeweled core
Discovered
Upon becoming
A labor of shedding
Casting aside
Detritus accumulated
By ancestors' ancestors' ancestors
Passed
To descendants' descendants' descendants
Until
Here
We take our stand
Joyfully
At the event horizon of human collapse
Shaking off
Laying down
Shrug and gone
Tears shed
Water usefully clearing
Maka piapia
Once clouding
Now clearing
From one to one to one
Innumerable ones

Until the entire earth sighs
Just ahead of sea level rise
We accept our covenant
With Mother Earth as she raised her head to the heavens
Kuleana undeniable
At long last
She laughs, even
Having waited sooooooooo
Long
Four thousand years in one direction
Cannot be righted in just
One generation
So let us count us as the first of many
Generations to come
Yes, we can dare to say
There will be
Generations to come
If
And only if
We undeniably answer the call
To the child and elder within us
Both true
Required, even
To evolve
As we must
Not in Darwinian epochs
Rather, in clear-eyed
Determination
Forged by our own hands
Given up to useful practice

Disconnecting overworked thumbs
And fleeting memes, screeds
Yada yada
No longer chasing the approval of strangers on phones
Extricating ourselves
And those we love
From the stew of our own mourning
Morning indeed calls us
Depends on us
Loves us
Greets us
In practice honing
Shedding
Setting aside
That which is no longer useful
In us
No use
To the present
And future
Humans being human
In communion
With all beings
Having done their part for us
Now is our time
(More than so!)
To usefully
Purposefully
Arise
In service of
Descendants' descendants' descendants
As

A Reflection

Ancestors' ancestors' ancestors
Would wish to be so
Sending fragments of prayers
From distant stars and underground spores
Dormant no longer
How could we be
Past the time of ripeness
And expiration dates for
Cynics, skeptics, whiners
This said without judgment
Just observation
Past the time
To pass the time
Litigating who is right and who is not
For
Wholeness is not an accommodation of our troubled existence
It is less than naught
In the subspace of useless arguments
Denying fills no hole in the middle of our heart
Our loss gives useful way
To resolve's hard-fought hope
To know and fill
From the cocoons of our own making
The isolation of I
Meeting the spirited warmth of we
As we raise our eyes to the horizon
Of a world we know can be
Will be
This we know with certainty
For we are telling the stories
From the darkness of Pō

To red dawn awakening
In fierce aloha
This enduring wind
Emergent beingness
Aloha

Notes

1 An event horizon is the boundary area of a black hole, where the gravitational pull is so strong that any object will be pulled into the black hole.

2 Pō is dark, darkness, night. Like all Indigenous people and scientists, Native Hawaiians observed the darkest part of the night occurring just before dawn.

3 "Don't listen with your ears, listen with your mind. No, don't listen with your mind, but listen with your spirit. Listening stops with the ears. The mind stops with recognition, but spirit is empty and waits on all things. The Way gathers in emptiness alone. Emptiness is the fasting of the mind." —Chuang Tzu, Taoist philosopher

4 The author has been a Rinzai Zen practitioner since the early 1980s. Her home temple is Daihonzan Chozen-ji in Kalihi Valley on the island of Oʻahu. She is the abbot of Anko-in, an independent branch temple of Chozen-ji, and supports with other teachers a far-flung sangha across the continental United States and eastern Canada.

5 "Maka piapia!" might be thrown as an insult for someone who doesn't see what they should be able to see.

6 Please don't send socks or tea. I have many socks; I have much tea. Plus, I'm picky.

7 This is Lao Tzu's and other Taoist philosophers' Virtue.

8 "... to hear what is not said, to see what cannot be seen, and to know the unknowable—that is Aloha" —Lili'uokalani, Native Hawaiian leader

Photo Credits

Pages 3 & 4: Suzanne Thomson, hands sculpted from clay; photos by Evan Penny and Julie Epp, March 2025.

Page 41: Naʻālehu Anthony, photo "Curiosity," October 2024.

Page 91: Ellanore Q, "Let Your Mind Blow Wild," a poem on a card when she was 7.5 years old; photo by Scott Nine, February 2018. With permission of the author and artist.

About the Author

 **Norma Ryūkō Kawelokū Wong Roshi**, familiarly known as Norma Wong or Wong Roshi, is an emerging kupuna (elder) living in the land of her birth, Hawaiʻi. She is of Hakka and Native Hawaiian ancestry. Her ancestors lived in the Hawaiian Islands centuries before Western contact. Earlier years were spent in community and policy work, and she served as a Hawaiʻi state legislator and as a policy advisor and strategist to former Governor John Waiheʻe. The term "Roshi" recognizes her responsibilities as an 86th generation Zen Master of the Rinzai Zen line. In addition to spiritual teaching, Norma has spent many years in the applied space—the direct application of Indigenous and Zen ways, values, and practices to living and transformational change critical to our times. *For more, please visit www.normawong.com.*

About North Atlantic Books

North Atlantic Books (NAB) is an independent, nonprofit publisher committed to a bold exploration of the relationships between mind, body, spirit, and nature. Founded in 1974, NAB aims to nurture a holistic view of the arts, sciences, humanities, and healing. To make a donation or to learn more about our books, authors, events, and newsletter, please visit *www.northatlanticbooks.com*.

BIBLIOGRAPHY

The following books helped me to plot a path for you through both swordsmanship and Zen. I have, of course, added my own thoughts and insights, but I have kept these to a minimum so as to maintain some academic rigour.

Books

Anshin, A., *The Truth of the Ancient Ways: A Critical Biography of the Swordsman Yamaoka Tesshu*. Kodenkan Institute, 2012

Arai, P. & K. Trainor, *Oxford Handbook of Buddhist Practice*. Oxford University Press, 2022

Bergland, C., *The Athlete's Way: Training Your Mind and Body to Experience the Joy of Exercise*. St Martin's Griffin, 2007

Dumoulin, H., *Zen Buddhism: A History: India and China*. World Wisdom, 2005

Fischer, N. & S. Moon, *What is Zen?: Plain Talk for a Beginner's Mind*. Shambhala Publications, 2016

Gladwell, M., *Blink: The Power of Thinking Without Thinking*. Little, Brown and Company, 2005

Halchak, Y. E., *Study of Japanese Swords: Chronological Study of Japanese Swords and Japanese History*. Alpha Books, 2021

Inagaki, H., *A Dictionary of Buddhist Terms, with Supplement* (fifth edition). Stone Bridge Press, 1992

King, W., *Zen and the Way of the Samurai Sword: Arming the Samurai Psyche*. Oxford University Press, 1993

Marapana, T., *The Mechanics of Buddhism*. Vijitha Yapa Publications, 2006

Nishitani, K., *On Buddhism*. State University of New York Press, 2006

Nukariya, K., *The Religion of the Samurai: A Study of Zen Philosophy and Discipline in China and Japan*. Bibliotech Press, 2023

Schuhmacher, S., *Zen in Plain English: Experience the Essence of Zen*. Watkins, 2009

Suzuki, D. T., *Zen and Japanese Culture*. Princeton University Press, 1970

Victoria, B. D., *Zen at War*. Rowman & Littlefield Publications Inc, 2006

Wilson, W. S., *The Life-Giving Sword: Secret Teachings from the House of the Shogun*. Kodansha, 2009

Wilson, W. S., *The Unfettered Mind: Writings from a Zen Master to a Master Swordsman*. Shambhala Publications, 2012

Wright, D. S., *The Six Perfections: Buddhism and Cultivation of Character*. Oxford University Press, 2009

Audio books

Dates and publishers relate to the audio editions.

Chodron, T., *Buddhism for Beginners*. Audible Studios, 2014

Cobb, I., *What is Zen*. Author's Republic, 2023

Davis, B. W., *Real Zen for Real Life*. The Great Courses, 2020

Eckel, M. D., *Buddhism*. The Great Courses, 2013

Landaw, J., S. Bodian & G. Bühnemann, *Buddhism for Dummies* (second edition). Tantor Audio, 2019

Nukariya, K., *The Religion of the Samurai: A Study of Zen Philosophy and Discipline in China and Japan*. Audible Studios, 2012

Skilton, A., *A Concise History of Buddhism: From 500BCE–1900CE*. Dharma Audiobooks from W. F. Howes Ltd, 2016

Suzuki, D. T., *An Introduction to Zen Buddhism*. W. F. Howes Ltd, 2023

Suzuki, D. T., *Zen and the Art of Tea*. Macmillan Audio, 2000

Suzuki, D. T., *Zen and the Samurai*. Macmillan Audio, 2003

Tanahashi, K., *Sky Above, Great Wind: The Life and Poetry of Zen Master Ryokan*. Audible Studios, 2014

Tanahashi, K. & P. Levitt (eds), *The Essential Dogen: Writings of the Great Zen Master*. Audible Studios, 2014